Gastric Bypass Surgery

EVERYTHING YOU
NEED TO KNOW TO MAKE AN
INFORMED DECISION

Gastric Bypass Surgery

Mary P. McGowan, M.D., with
Jo McGowan Chopra

McGraw·Hill

New York   Chicago   San Francisco   Lisbon   London   Madrid   Mexico City
Milan   New Delhi   San Juan   Seoul   Singapore   Sydney   Toronto

Library of Congress Cataloging-in-Publication Data

McGowan, Mary P., 1959–
     Gastric bypass surgery : everything you need to know to make an informed
decision / Mary P. McGowan, with Jo McGowan Chopra ; foreword by Connie J.
Campbell.
        p.   cm.
     ISBN 0-07-143192-6 (alk. paper)
     1. Gastric bypass—Popular works.   I. McGowan Chopra, Jo.   II. Title.

RD540.5.M38   2004
616.3'9806—dc22   2003022340

1 2 3 4 5 6 7 8 9 0   DOC/DOC   3 2 1 0 9 8 7 6 5 4

ISBN 0-07-143192-6

McGraw-Hill books are available at special quantity discounts to use as premiums and
sales promotions, or for use in corporate training programs. For more information,
please write to the Director of Special Sales, Professional Publishing, McGraw-Hill,
Two Penn Plaza, New York, NY 10121-2298. Or contact your local bookstore.

This book is printed on acid-free paper.

To the staff and patients of the Obesity Treatment
Center at Catholic Medical Center in
Manchester, New Hampshire.

Contents

Foreword

Obesity shortens your life. Medical research documents the many diseases that develop more frequently in obese individuals. A recent study revealed the direct correlation between obesity and a shortened lifespan. For example, a twenty-year-old obese white man has a lifespan thirteen years less than a twenty-year-old of normal weight. Weight loss is actually a common prescription for disorders like high blood pressure, high cholesterol, heart disease, diabetes, sleep apnea, infertility, heartburn, and in preparation for hernia repair and joint replacement.

The highest health risks are associated with being morbidly obese, that is, being one hundred pounds overweight or having a body mass index (BMI) of 40 or greater. Morbidly obese individuals may have temporary success in losing the large amount of weight required to make themselves healthier, but long-term even those people who are capable of significant weight loss are generally not able to keep the weight off unless they have had surgery. In 1991, the National Institutes of Health (NIH) issued a consensus statement recommending gastric bypass surgery for individuals with a BMI of 40 or higher, or a BMI of 35 or higher with one or more obesity-related medical problems, who had failed to benefit from traditional weight loss methods. Gastric bypass surgery can help people lose such significant amounts of weight that patients can actually be cured of their obesity-related medical problems. Ninety-eight percent of diabetics that have bariatric surgery no longer need any diabetic medications. Ninety-eight percent of people are also cured of sleep apnea and gastroesophageal reflux. Ninety-two percent of patients with high blood pressure go into remission.

Gastric bypass surgery results in a very serious, permanent change to the body. For some people, it provides an excellent tool with which to lose and keep off significant amounts of weight. Such permanent weight loss literally adds years to their life. The results of gastric bypass surgery can not only improve the quantity of life, but also the quality of life. Imagine, no more insulin injections. No more sleeping with a C-PAP apparatus. No more embarrassing moments trying to fit into an airplane seat. Imagine, self-confidence and self-esteem.

However, weight loss surgery is not for everyone. Before deciding on gastric bypass, you must examine the underlying psychological and social circumstances that contribute to your obesity so that you are prepared for all the lifestyle changes you will have to make postoperatively. You will need to commit to a healthy recovery from the surgery. It takes focus to follow the strict diet that will be necessary so that you do not harm the stomach pouch, and consequently yourself. You will need to determine if you can commit to a lifetime of caring for your rerouted digestive system. This book focuses on questions that patients must answer for themselves to help determine whether or not gastric bypass is an appropriate option for them.

As a cholesterol management specialist at the New England Heart Institute, Dr. McGowan is often in the position of evaluating morbidly obese patients who have just experienced their first heart attack. She knows that if they do not lose significant amounts of weight, they are likely to die an early death. Dr. McGowan began to recommend gastric bypass surgery to select individuals and saw the success that these patients had. However, she became frustrated by the lack of availability of this procedure. Her patients had to travel to Boston, where they ended up on a waiting list for a couple of years until there was room for them on the surgeon's schedule. After dealing with one too many disappointed patients, she asked me if I would consider putting a program together here in Manchester, New Hampshire. As I began to look into bariatric surgery, I realized that there was a tremendous need for this type of service in our community. The surgeons at Boston's New England Medical Center offered to share their technical expertise with me since they saw the benefit of the procedure but were overwhelmed by the volume of patients requiring it. After much research and many meetings, the Obesity Treatment Center at Catholic Medical Center came into being.

As we were developing the Center, Dr. McGowan and her partner, Carolyn Finocchario, put together a list of interested patients who would benefit from this procedure. At the same time, Dr. McGowan was starting to see the dramatic results that her patients were having after undergoing bariatric surgery. Their cholesterol levels were perfect. They no longer required blood pressure medication. They felt more energetic and were exercising more. Dr. McGowan wanted other people to know of the successes of bariatric surgery so that they might consider it for themselves. After all, being the ideal body weight comes in at number four on the ways to lower cholesterol in Dr. McGowan's book *50 Ways to Lower Your Cholesterol.*

Gastric Bypass Surgery is an excellent compilation of facts, information, and advice for anyone who is considering gastric bypass surgery. Dr. McGowan and her coauthor and sister Jo McGowan Chopra are both superb educators who have thoughtfully outlined many of the physiologic, nutritional, and psychological issues surrounding gastric bypass surgery. They outline the NIH recommendations regarding who should consider the surgery and detail the individual considerations that patients have shared with Dr. McGowan as they go through the decision-making process. They tell you how to maximize the success of the surgery and minimize the complications. And in a very practical section, they include sample letters to help persuade your insurance company to cover the surgery. The authors include the recommendations of our nutritionist, Jacquie Cuddihy, for both preoperative and postoperative meal planning, and there are even sample menus. Dr. McGowan outlines a postoperative, long-term health maintenance plan involving sensible eating and exercise, and the book includes a Glossary and an excellent Bibliography.

This book is a wonderful resource for anyone considering gastric bypass surgery as well as for their family and friends. I am grateful that Dr. McGowan and Jo McGowan Chopra have provided such an accurate, straightforward, and comprehensive guide to the gastric bypass experience so that I can recommend it to my patients.

Connie J. Campbell, M.D., F.A.C.S.

Acknowledgments

Two years ago I spoke to Dr. Connie Campbell about the need for a gastric bypass program in Manchester, New Hampshire. At that time I was sending my patients either to Boston, Massachusetts (New England Medical Center), or Lebanon, New Hampshire (Dartmouth—Mary Hitchcock Medical Center). While they all received excellent care at these centers, many complained about the distance they had to travel. Connie, a gifted surgeon with extensive experience performing laparoscopic surgery, agreed that a local program was necessary.

She and I approached Alyson Pitman Giles, the CEO of our hospital, who after listening carefully to us agreed that such a program would likely benefit our community. Like any good CEO, however, she told us that in order to develop the program we would have to do a true needs assessment (it wasn't enough to just *feel* that the community needed this program), and we would then have to convince her that our proposed program would not lose money.

The needs assessment proved our assumption correct. Manchester did require a gastric bypass program. Over the next few months we held meetings with the financial and administrative leaders of the hospital (George Allen, Ray Benito, Lisa Drouse, Scott Colby, Darlene Stromstad, and Patsy Aprile). Clinical staff members (Denise McGlone, Melanie Davis, Lisa Haeger, Jacquie Cuddihy, and Bob Duhaime) were also actively involved in determining the best way to develop our program. Alyson insisted on excellence as well as thrift. If we were going to do it, we were going to do it properly, but we would have to be creative and budget-conscious.

The program would require a medical director, a surgical director (we knew that would be Connie), a nutritionist, a psychologist, and a nurse practitioner (who would oversee the entire program). Things soon came together.

Dr. Lisa Haeger, an old friend from medical school, had just moved to New Hampshire after many years in California. She joined our medical staff and took on the job as medical director. Both Lisa and Connie benefited greatly from the expertise of Drs. Edward Saltzman and Scott Shikora at the New England Medical Center, who offered advice on program development. In developing the program Connie spent a significant amount of time in Massachusetts performing surgery with the New England Medical Center team.

Jacquie Cuddihy is an outstanding nutritionist with many years of experience, who embraced the challenge of learning everything she could about the dietary requirements before and after gastric bypass. She spent over a year researching and is now truly an expert. Megan Griffiths, a wonderful psychiatric nurse practitioner, soon joined the team. Megan brings a wealth of psychological experience to the program. Melanie Davis was selected to be the nurse practitioner and director of the program. Melanie is passionate about her job and always available for her patients. She has created an environment where patients feel at home and often develop close supportive relationships with each other.

In fact, everyone at the Obesity Treatment Center is passionate about his or her job—the staff members work beautifully with each other and with the patients. It is truly a wonderful team. One very special aspect of the program is that both Megan and Melanie have themselves had a gastric bypass procedure. While neither spends a great deal of time talking about her own story, they both speak openly about it to patients. Somehow patients feel less alone when they learn this.

I am truly indebted to the administrative staff at Catholic Medical Center and to the Obesity Treatment Center team for providing a much needed service to our community. I am also grateful to Cynthia David for her assistance in obtaining the hundreds of research articles I reviewed in preparing this book. I would also like to acknowledge my own staff (Mary Card, Katie Demers, Carolyn Finocchario, Diane Hebert, Kristie Lloyd, Susan Lynch, Marisse Mauricio, Betty Ouellette, and Zena Ligon) for their endless support during this project.

It is to my patients, however, that I owe my greatest debt. Their courage in undergoing major and life-changing surgery has been an inspiration to all of us who work with them. Their willingness to speak openly about their own lives and the adjustments and struggles they have encountered has made me a better doctor. It is because of their stories that I was able to write this book.

Finally my thanks to my husband, Tom, and our children, Patrick, Liam, and Sheila, whose patience allowed me to write this book. Tom, I promise no more books for a while.

Introduction

You have picked up this book because you want to lose weight. You've tried every weight loss program there is, and, as with most overweight people, while some of those programs have worked for a while, in the end the weight has always come back. You want something permanent. Weight loss surgery is a daunting decision, and a bit frightening, too, but it is undoubtedly the most effective approach to long-term enduring weight loss.

As you consider weight loss surgery, you will have many questions. In my practice as a physician who treats people with obesity-related illnesses, I have helped many people navigate the sea of scientific jargon and bewildering procedures that this process entails. Most of my patients have the same questions. This book will give you the answers you need to make the right decision.

But before you consider weight loss surgery, there are two questions you need to ask yourself:

1. Are you, in fact, a candidate for such a procedure?
   Although your weight is the major factor deter-

mining your eligibility for weight loss surgery, your medical and psychological history are important as well. In order to determine if you weigh enough to consider weight loss surgery you will need to know your body mass index (BMI). This is a way of looking at weight in relation to height. The very first question in this book deals with this. In addition to determining BMI, certain medical and psychological conditions must be considered when reviewing candidacy. This too is discussed fully in the next few pages.

2. Are you emotionally prepared for such a dramatic and life-changing intervention? This is a less easily defined issue, and there is no "emotional mass index" chart I can give you to help you make the decision. As you read this book, you will ask yourself some difficult questions. Exploring and answering these questions fully will prepare you for what lies ahead. I firmly believe that emotional preparation improves a person's postoperative course.

If, after careful consideration of these two factors, you decide to go forward, you will need to find a bariatric (weight loss) surgery program in your area. This book will direct you to sources of up-to-date information on those programs in your area. Will your insurance plan pay for the procedure? While many companies say no at first, there are ways of getting it covered. If you do qualify for weight loss surgery, this book will help you formulate a letter to your insurance provider stating your case.

Once you have coverage for your surgery you will most likely be required to go through a program of education, diet, and psychological counseling. While this might seem like an unnecessary delay now, by the time you have read this book you will understand why proceeding slowly and preparing thoroughly is crucial. Although nothing can completely prepare you for the experience, the more knowledgeable you are, the more smoothly it will go.

There are a number of different bariatric procedures. This book will discuss the various options including the popular Roux-en-Y procedure, vertical-banded gastroplasty, biliopancreatic diversion with duodenal switch, and gastric banding. You and your physician will work together to determine which procedure is right for you.

While gastric surgery is a choice that will change your life dramatically, it is also a surgical procedure like any other. You will want to know how long you will take to heal and what potential complications to be prepared for. You will want to know how soon you will be able to eat and what foods you will be able to tolerate. You will want to know when you can move from liquids to purees and then on to solids. While each patient is a unique individual and every program is different, this book will help you with general guidelines on the rate of progression.

You may not have thought much about how gastric surgery will change some of your personal relationships. Many overweight people surround themselves with overweight friends—people they eat with and who help them define who they are. Some of your friends and family members may be jealous of, and threatened by, your weight loss. You need to be prepared for this. If you sense this could become a problem it may be best to discuss these issues with your friends and family now. This book will give you ideas for opening what could be a very delicate conversation.

Along with your personal relationships, your relationship to food will also be entirely transformed. Family gatherings, holiday celebrations, even simple lunch dates will be very different once the quantity you can consume is so strictly limited. And since secret bingeing will no longer be a possibility either, you will need to understand clearly the compulsions that contributed to your overeating in the first place.

Finally, I imagine the most important thing you want to know is how much weight you can expect to lose. Not only will this book give you the answer, it will also give you guidance on how to maximize your weight loss. By reading this book you are showing initiative in seeking improved health and well-being for yourself. The answers to all of these questions will help you prepare to make the decision whether gastric bypass surgery is for you, as well as to obtain the best possible results if you choose this option. We wish you good health.

CHAPTER ONE

Am I a Candidate?

Should I have weight loss surgery? Every time I turn around I read about another celebrity who has lost one hundred–plus pounds with weight loss surgery. I can't help but wonder if I might be a candidate for this procedure. How do doctors decide who qualifies and who doesn't?

The first thing your doctor might do as he or she decides if you are a candidate for weight loss surgery (also called bariatric surgery) is to determine your body mass index, or BMI (see Figure 1.1 and Table 1.1). The BMI is determined by converting your weight in pounds to kilograms and your height in inches to meters and is defined as your weight in kilograms divided by your height in meters squared (kg/m^2). You can calculate your own BMI by dividing your weight in pounds by your height in inches; divide the number obtained by your height in inches (yes, you divide by your height in inches twice); then multiply this number by 703. The final figure is your BMI.

FIGURE 1.1 Body Mass Index Chart

BMI	19	20	21	22	23	24	25	26	27	28	29	30	31	32	33	34	35	36	37	38	39	40	41	42	43	44	45	46	47	48	49	50	51	52	53	54
Height (inches)												**Body Weight (pounds)**																								
58	91	96	100	105	110	115	119	124	129	134	138	143	148	153	158	162	167	172	177	181	186	191	196	201	205	210	215	220	224	229	234	239	244	248	253	258
59	94	99	104	109	114	119	124	128	133	138	143	148	153	158	163	168	173	178	183	188	193	198	203	208	212	217	222	227	232	237	242	247	252	257	262	267
60	97	102	107	112	118	123	128	133	138	143	148	153	158	163	168	174	179	184	189	194	199	204	209	215	220	225	230	235	240	245	250	255	261	266	271	276
61	100	106	111	116	122	127	132	137	143	148	153	158	164	169	174	180	185	190	195	201	206	211	217	222	227	232	238	243	248	254	259	264	269	275	280	285
62	104	109	115	120	126	131	136	142	147	153	158	164	169	175	180	186	191	196	202	207	213	218	224	229	235	240	246	251	256	262	267	273	278	284	289	295
63	107	113	118	124	130	135	141	146	152	158	163	169	175	180	186	191	197	203	208	214	220	225	231	237	242	248	254	259	265	270	278	282	287	293	299	304
64	110	116	122	128	134	140	145	151	157	163	169	174	180	186	192	197	204	209	215	221	227	232	238	244	250	256	262	267	273	279	285	291	296	302	308	314
65	114	120	126	132	138	144	150	156	162	168	174	180	186	192	198	204	210	216	222	228	234	240	246	252	258	264	270	276	282	288	294	300	306	312	318	324
66	118	124	130	136	142	148	155	161	167	173	179	186	192	198	204	210	216	223	229	235	241	247	253	260	266	272	278	284	291	297	303	309	315	322	328	334
67	121	127	134	140	146	153	159	166	172	178	185	191	198	204	211	217	223	230	236	242	249	255	261	268	274	280	287	293	299	306	312	319	325	331	338	344
68	125	131	138	144	151	158	164	171	177	184	190	197	203	210	216	223	230	236	243	249	256	262	269	276	282	289	295	302	308	315	322	328	335	341	348	354
69	128	135	142	149	155	162	169	176	182	189	196	203	209	216	223	230	236	243	250	257	263	270	277	284	291	297	304	311	318	324	331	338	345	351	358	365
70	132	139	146	153	160	167	174	181	188	195	202	209	216	222	229	236	243	250	257	264	271	278	285	292	299	306	313	320	327	334	341	348	355	362	369	376
71	136	143	150	157	165	172	179	186	193	200	208	215	222	229	236	243	250	257	265	272	279	286	293	301	308	315	322	329	338	343	351	358	365	372	379	386
72	140	147	154	162	169	177	184	191	199	206	213	221	228	235	242	250	258	265	272	279	287	294	302	309	316	324	331	338	346	353	361	368	375	383	390	397
73	144	151	159	166	174	182	189	197	204	212	219	227	235	242	250	257	265	272	280	288	295	302	310	318	325	333	340	348	355	363	371	378	386	393	401	408
74	148	155	163	171	179	186	194	202	210	218	225	233	241	249	256	264	272	280	287	295	303	311	319	326	334	342	350	358	365	373	381	389	396	404	412	420
75	152	160	168	176	184	192	200	208	216	224	232	240	248	256	264	272	279	287	295	303	311	319	327	335	343	351	359	367	375	383	391	399	407	415	423	431
76	156	164	172	180	189	197	205	213	221	230	238	246	254	263	271	279	287	295	304	312	320	328	336	344	353	361	369	377	385	394	402	410	418	426	435	443

Source: Adapted from Clinical Guidelines on the Identification, Evaluation, and Treatment of Overweight and Obesity in Adults: The Evidence Report.

TABLE 1.1 BMI Chart

Category	BMI
Underweight	< 18.5
Normal	18.5–24.9
Overweight	25–29.9
Class I Obesity	30–34.9
Class II Obesity	35–39.9
Class III Obesity	≥ 40

In general, weight loss surgery is considered for people with Class II obesity if they have obesity-related illnesses and Class III obesity with or without related illnesses.

What is an "obesity-related illness"?

Obesity-related illnesses and conditions include elevated cholesterol and triglycerides, gallstones, pancreatitis, abdominal hernia, fatty liver, diabetes and prediabetes, polycystic ovary syndrome, high blood pressure, heart disease, pulmonary hypertension, stroke, blood clots in the legs and lungs, sleep apnea, arthritis, gout, lower back pain, infertility, urinary incontinence, and cataracts. If you have one of these conditions gastric surgery can be considered when the BMI is 35 or higher. In many cases gastric bypass surgery can dramatically improve obesity-related conditions. I have had many patients who after gastric bypass surgery were able to give up their blood pressure, diabetes, and cholesterol lowering medications. Many young women who have been unable to become pregnant conceive and go on to have healthy babies (more on this later).

What other factors are used to determine if a person is a good candidate for bariatric surgery?

For most people, BMI is the most important factor. However, your doctor needs to carefully consider your current physical and emotional health as well. For example, if you have recently had cancer treatment, major surgery, a heart attack, or a cardiac procedure, your doctor may feel that you should wait a period of time before considering bariatric surgery.

With regard to emotional health, people with a history of anorexia nervosa are generally not considered good candidates for this surgery. Likewise, uncontrolled bulimia (self-induced vomiting, typically following binge eating) is generally a contraindication for bariatric surgery. If you have had an eating disorder in the past but have been well controlled for a long time, your doctor may consider you a good candidate.

Finally, if you have long-standing psychiatric difficulties such as schizophrenia or manic depression you are unlikely to be a good candidate for weight loss surgery. I would like to emphasize that these criteria are simply rules of thumb; nothing is in stone. Each person has a unique set of circumstances. The final decision is ultimately up to you, your personal physician, and your bariatric surgeon.

Are there any age requirements for gastric bypass surgery?

Until about a year ago gastric bypass surgery was almost exclusively an adult surgery. There is a growing recognition, however, that the obesity epidemic in this country also includes children. Many obese children develop "adult" diseases or conditions such as high blood pressure, type 2 diabetes, and high cholesterol. Obese children are often taunted and teased by their peers. Clearly, obesity can take a physical and emotional toll on the young. Because of these concerns a few centers in the United States are offering this surgery to carefully selected teens. In general surgeons wait until a teen has achieved adult height. For young women this is typically by thirteen or fourteen years of age, and for young men by fifteen or sixteen. As this book goes to press guidelines for selecting appropriate pediatric candidates for gastric bypass surgery are being drafted.

I have had a problem with binge eating. Does this mean I am not a candidate for bariatric surgery?

The short answer to this question is that gastric bypass surgery may actually be thought of as a treatment for binge eating. Binge eating disorder (BED) has been reported in as many as 68 percent of people undergoing gastric bypass surgery. Interestingly, some people who think they have BED really do not. In order to meet the strict definition of BED, episodes of binge eating must occur at least two days a week for a period of about six months. In addition to consuming large amounts of food over a period of about two hours, binge eaters describe a sense of loss of control. In other words they cannot stop themselves, nor do they feel in control of what or how much they are consuming.

Most binge eaters also describe eating very quickly and feeling very full. Binge eaters usually eat alone and are very distressed by their own behavior. Unlike people with bulimia, binge eaters do not vomit, and unlike people with anorexia nervosa they do not fast or exercise to excess to make up for the bingeing. While your doctor should be told of your BED, it is unlikely to preclude bariatric surgery.

It is important to point out that people with BED often have underlying depression. Sometimes treating the underlying condition with antidepressants dramatically improves BED. If depression is diagnosed, treatment should begin before undergoing surgery. Other beneficial therapies for BED include cognitive therapy and bariatric surgery.

Why am I so overweight? I know that I overeat and that I don't exercise enough. But there must be more to it because I know some people whose habits are far worse than mine and they are thin.

You are absolutely right, severe obesity is often more than just too many calories and too little exercise. In each person the exact cause of severe obesity is different. Scientists believe that obesity is due to the complex interplay of genetics, environment, and culture. A person's psychological makeup also plays a role in the development of obesity. It is far too simple to say that obesity is just a matter of poor self-control and lack of exercise. Any person with severe obesity has a chronic illness that may require surgery and certainly will require lifelong medical and possibly psychological care.

The current environment in the United States fosters obesity. Everywhere you turn there is a fast food restaurant where cheap, high-fat, high-calorie food abounds, and it is all too easy to ask the clerk behind the counter to "super-size" it. When we do this we are "super-sizing" ourselves. If you have gastric bypass surgery you will have to work hard to change your environment and your habits. In fact, you should strike the phrase "super-size" from your vocabulary.

I think I am a good candidate for gastric bypass surgery. What do I need to do to obtain insurance coverage for this procedure?

Unfortunately, it is not enough for you to think you will be a good candidate for surgery: you must also meet the National Institutes of Health guidelines for surgical eligibility. These guidelines state that candidates for obesity surgery must have:

1. A BMI of 40 or more, or in some cases a BMI of 35 or more in association with one or more major obesity-related medical or physical problems.
2. Failed all previous attempts at weight reduction by conventional means (diet, exercise, counseling, and weight loss medications).
3. No history of alcohol or substance abuse.
4. Realistic expectations of surgical outcome.

If you meet these guidelines, the next step is a visit to your primary care doctor to discuss surgery. If you have the type of insurance that requires a referral, you will need your primary care doctor to refer you to a surgeon. Your doctor should also write a letter of support on your behalf to your insurance company. If you have a long-standing relationship with your primary care doctor, he or she will know about your weight loss attempts and will be treating you for any of your obesity-related illnesses or conditions (elevated cholesterol and triglycerides, gallstones, pancreatitis, abdominal hernia, fatty liver, diabetes or prediabetes, polycystic ovary syndrome, high blood pressure, heart disease, pulmonary hypertension, stroke, blood clots in the legs and lungs, sleep apnea, arthritis, gout, lower back pain, infertility, urinary incontinence, or cataracts).

If you do not have a long-term relationship with your doctor you should bring detailed notes to give her or him. These should include information on specific diets you have been on, when you were on the diet, and how successful you were. If you did lose weight during any of your weight loss attempts, you should supply your doctor with information on how long you were able to maintain it. Your primary care doctor should be aware of your obesity-related conditions, but if you have seen specialists for various problems, he or she might not have all the details of treatments you have received. If you want your procedure to be approved quickly, I suggest you draft a sample letter for your physician. (See Appendix B for an example of a sample letter.)

It is important to remember that many physicians have pretty healthy egos. You know your doctor (I don't). If you think your doctor would be insulted by you giving him or her a sample letter, think of a different way to phrase it. You might explain that you have researched the requirements of your particular insurance company and know that in order to avoid immediate claim rejection, certain things need to be included in a letter of support. Most physicians have had enough negative experiences with rejected claims that they will be happy that you have researched the claims process of your particular insurance company and that their time is less likely to be wasted. Physicians are also very busy—if you have drafted a good letter it is very likely that your doctor will dictate it nearly verbatim.

While a letter from your primary care doctor is helpful, the most important thing he or she can do for you is refer you to a good surgeon. It is important for you to be aware of the surgeons in your area who perform bariatric surgery. Since bariatric surgery has only recently become commonplace, your doctor may not know who performs this type of surgery in your community. If your doctor refuses to refer you and you know you qualify (see the NIH criteria above), then you need to find a new primary care physician.

If you have to go this route, make sure that the new doctor you select has at least referred a few patients for this procedure. You can get this information from various sources. One way to find a doctor likely to refer you is to call the office of the surgeon you hope to have do your procedure and ask which local doctors refer to him or her. You might also attend a support group or informational seminar and ask the patients present who their doctors are. Once you have a primary doctor in mind call the office and ask if he or she is accepting new patients. If the answer is yes, schedule an appointment.

Hopefully things will go smoothly for you and your current doctor will immediately refer you to a surgeon, but if this doesn't happen don't give up—find a new doctor who will make the referral.

Once referred, your surgeon's letter is generally the most important piece of information used by your insurance company. It is important to supply your surgeon with the same information you supplied to your primary care physician.

Your surgeon and his or her office staff will most likely be very experienced with writing the detailed letters of medical necessity. Often you will be asked to complete a formal questionnaire. These questionnaires usually include questions regarding your dieting attempts and your obesity-related conditions. Sometimes they include questions regarding the social and economic consequences you may have experienced related to your weight. All of this information will be used in your letter of medical necessity, so be honest and complete.

No one is more invested than you in obtaining insurance approval. And ultimately insurance coverage is your responsibility, so be proactive. Once you know your surgeon has submitted all the necessary paperwork to your insurance company, wait one to two weeks, then call the insurance company to check on the status of your case. Sometimes companies find trite problems with the application that hold up the process. One of my patients was unnecessarily delayed because the insurance company demanded additional proof that he had worked on a diet for a full year prior to seeking approval for coverage for weight loss surgery. Luckily I had clear documentation in his chart and was able to provide this information.

Bariatric surgery is becoming routine and is generally highly successful. As a result, more insurance companies are covering it. Nonetheless, many companies still make it painful. Some will deny coverage for any weight loss surgery, and they count on many people failing to appeal the ruling. If you are denied, don't give up—appeal the decision. Appendix C is a sample appeal letter. Obviously you will need to tailor it to your own situation, but this gives you an idea of what to include. You may also consider hiring a lawyer to handle the appeal for you.

I had one patient who successfully pitted one insurance company against another. My patient was covered under her own insurance plan and under her husband's plan as well. When her company refused coverage, her husband called his company and was told that coverage would be provided. His insurance company then told him that it would sue his wife's company for coverage. Miraculously his wife's company changed its ruling and the procedure was covered.

Most people are not in the lucky situation of having coverage with two insurance companies. If you are denied coverage, take a deep breath and get ready to fight. If you really do fit the NIH eligibility criteria, you should ultimately be successful.

As a way to boost your chances of immediate approval by your insurance company, I advise asking some of your other physicians to also write a letter of support to your insurance company. This might include your pulmonary doctor (if you have any obesity-related lung problems such as sleep apnea); your endocrinologist (if you have diabetes or polycystic ovary syndrome); your obstetrician-gynecologist (if you have obesity-related infertility or menstrual problems); your cardiologist (if you have obesity-related heart problems including an enlarged heart, high blood pressure, high cholesterol, a history of heart disease). The more support letters you have, the harder it is for your insurance company to deny you coverage.

If you find that your insurance policy specifically states that it does not cover treatment for weight loss and obesity, read between the lines. This usually means you are not covered for obesity medications or dietary counseling for the treatment of obesity. Weight loss surgery is a treatment for morbid obesity and is in a category of its own. It is important that you are aware of this distinction because many insurance companies will not point this exclusion out and hope you will go away.

Finally, although it may mean you have to wait a bit to qualify for gastric bypass surgery, you may need to change insurance companies. I have had a few patients who have done this in order to get coverage. Often employers only allow employees to change insurance plans (assuming they offer more than one option) once a year. You might need to discuss your situation with the human resources department at work. If you are lucky enough to have two or three options for insurance through your employer you will probably be able to find one company that will cover your procedure.

Another alternative, if you are married and your spouse could provide you with coverage, is to determine if making the switch would provide coverage for weight loss surgery. Still another (although more drastic) choice is to change jobs—but only do this if you know the new job will provide you with coverage for gastric bypass. If you have to go this route, once again you may be delayed as you accrue sick leave.

The last and least desirable option is the self-pay option. You may well have enough to cover the cost of an uncomplicated gastric bypass surgery. However you might not have an uncomplicated procedure. You might have complications that extend your time in the hospital or require a second trip to the operating room. In such a case the cost can really skyrocket.

Being forced to delay your surgery for insurance reasons may seem very frustrating at the moment, but try hard to remain upbeat. In the big scheme of things the timing of your surgery is not nearly as important as having it in the first place.

Melanie remembers being overweight as far back as kindergarten. Although a trained nurse who knew about nutrition and the importance of a well-balanced diet, her own life was a constant struggle to lose weight. She participated in medically supervised diets—from high-fiber to modified fasts—as well as trying every new fad diet on the market, but all without lasting success. At her peak she weighed 310 pounds, and she never saw below 200.

Melanie is smart, articulate, and hardworking, but she couldn't help but notice that despite these attributes, people treated her differently because of her weight. It was obvious to her that obesity was a handicap. "People immediately judge you—they think you are not ambitious, not hardworking."

After talking to her cousin, who knew someone who lost 100 pounds in six months due to gastric bypass surgery, Melanie wanted to consider it but assumed she could never afford the procedure. After researching the program and talking more with her cousin Melanie discovered that the procedure would be covered under her insurance plan. Melanie figured her BMI at 52—solidly in the range required for the surgery. She counted her blessings that she hadn't yet had any complications related to her weight, but at nearly forty, she knew that statistically it wouldn't be long before problems arose.

After waiting on an almost yearlong waiting list for the surgery, Melanie's day came. She shed 120 pounds. As can happen to many people, over the course of the next year she gained about 10 pounds back. She is working hard at losing them again. Melanie makes sure she walks thirty to forty minutes a day and tries to avoid snacking between meals, and is now working as the program director of Catholic Medical Center's Obesity Treatment Center in Manchester, New Hampshire, inspiring and supporting patients and physicians.

CHAPTER TWO

What to Expect from GBS

Types of Procedures and How They Work

How exactly does weight loss surgery promote weight loss?

It might help to consider the role of the stomach and small intestine in the normal situation. When you eat something it enters your esophagus and travels into your stomach. When food leaves the stomach it enters the small intestine, which is composed of three distinct parts. The first part of the small intestine is the duodenum, followed by the jejunum and the ileum. Each section has a specific role. In the stomach, iron and vitamin B_{12} are absorbed. The three parts of the small intestine are the powerhouses in terms of calorie and nutrient absorption. In addition, most of the absorption of vitamin D and calcium occurs in the duodenum and first portion of the jejunum.

There are two types of weight loss surgery—restrictive and malabsorptive. In restrictive surgery, the size of the stomach is dramatically reduced. This type of surgery makes a person very full, very fast. Overeating results in a very unpleasant feeling and often vomiting. After a restrictive procedure, weight loss is the result of not being able to consume calories.

In malabsorptive surgery, a large portion of the small intestine is bypassed, making the food you eat pass through only a part of the small intestine. Weight loss following this type of procedure is the result of an inability to absorb calories. This is because food does not come in contact with the bypassed portion of the small intestine. Although malabsorptive surgery can result in tremendous weight loss, it does have some drawbacks. I will discuss the pros and cons of each type of procedure in the next few pages.

The most popular weight loss surgery, Roux-en-Y procedure, is both restrictive and malabsorptive and will be discussed a little later.

Why or how does GBS result in permanent weight loss?

Bariatric surgery may allow weight loss in ways above and beyond just making the stomach much smaller and/or bypassing a portion of the small intestine. Some scientists believe that weight loss following bariatric surgery is also the result of diminished blood levels of a recently discovered hormone called ghrelin, which is secreted by endocrine cells within the stomach. Blood ghrelin levels rise prior to meals and in the face of food restriction or starvation.

A May 2002 article in the *New England Journal of Medicine* authored by Dr. David Cummings of the University of Washington reported that in obese people who lost weight through dietary changes, ghrelin levels rose quite substantially prior to meals. In contrast, people who lost a similar amount of weight following gastric bypass surgery were noted to have blood ghrelin levels 72 percent lower than matched obese controls. In addition people who underwent gastric bypass were not found to have spikes in ghrelin levels before meals. Since an increase in blood ghrelin is a potent stimulus to eat, this reduction in ghrelin level may be very important in the success of gastric bypass.

Cummings and his colleagues postulate that one of the reasons weight loss diets fail to be successful in the long run in obese people is that ghrelin levels spike prior to meals, prompting eating and regaining of any lost weight. This of course remains to be proven. Gastric bypass is known to cause weight loss because it makes your stomach smaller and causes a small reduction in your ability to absorb calories. Where ghrelin fits in still requires a great deal of research. If, however, ghrelin is found to be important you can be sure that pharmaceutical companies will try to develop medications to block its impact. Until then, I think gastric bypass is clearly the best approach for long-term weight loss in very obese people.

I have determined that I may be a candidate for bariatric surgery. How many different types of procedures are there?

There are four major weight loss procedures. These include vertical-banded gastroplasty, gastric banding, biliopancreatic diversion with duodenal switch, and the most commonly used Roux-en-Y procedure. The pictures that follow will help you understand the goal of each procedure.

As noted earlier, these surgical procedures either make the stomach very small (restrictive procedures), bypass much of the small intestine (malabsorptive), or combine both techniques. The most commonly used and, in my opinion, the safest, is the Roux-en-Y procedure. However, because there are circumstances where the other procedures might be most appropriate, I will describe each one.

Tell me about the restrictive procedures.

Vertical-banded gastroplasty and gastric banding are purely restrictive procedures (see Figures 2.1 and 2.2). In vertical-banded gastroplasty (Figure 2.1), the stomach is stapled fairly close to where the esophagus (food tube) meets the stomach. The staples are placed in a vertical fashion and a polypropylene (plastic) band is placed near the bottom of

FIGURE 2.1 Vertical-Banded Gastroplasty

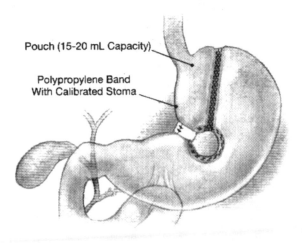

Pouch (15-20 mL Capacity)

Polypropylene Band
With Calibrated Stoma

Source: JAMA, December 11, 2002—Vol. 288, No. 22, p. 2794. Illustrated by C. Lynn. Reprinted with permission. Note: 5 mL = 1 teaspoon; 2.54 cm = 1 inch.

the staple line. As can be seen from the drawing, the stapling results in a very small stomach while the band restricts how quickly food can leave this reduced pouch.

Does vertical-banded gastroplasty result in any vitamin or mineral deficiencies?

In the stomach food comes in contact with gastric acid. Iron found in foods such as spinach, raisins, and red meat requires contact with gastric acid to convert it from the ferrous form, which is not readily absorbed, to the ferric form, which is. If iron is not absorbed adequately, anemia can result. The stomach also contains something called intrinsic factor, which aids in the absorption of vitamin B_{12}. Vitamin

FIGURE 2.2 Gastric Banding

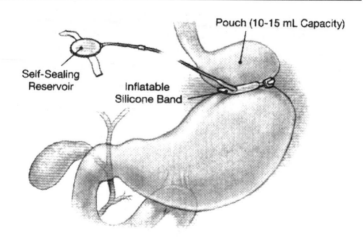

Source: JAMA, December 11, 2002—Vol. 288, No. 22, p. 2794. Illustrated by C. Lynn. Reprinted with permission. Note: 5 mL = 1 teaspoon; 2.54 cm = 1 inch.

B$_{12}$ deficiency can result in a condition called pernicious anemia. Vertical-banded gastroplasty can result in a deficiency of both iron and vitamin B$_{12}$. Although this is generally not a major problem, supplements of both iron and vitamin B$_{12}$ are usually necessary. Because of the potential for vitamin and mineral deficiencies following gastric bypass surgery, it is crucial for you to maintain regular follow-up with the nurses, doctors, and dietitians at your gastric bypass center.

Do people keep their weight off following vertical-banded gastroplasty?

While initial weight loss is quite good with vertical-banded gastroplasty, long-term maintenance is poor. Unlike most other forms of gastric bypass surgery, following vertical-banded gastroplasty most people are not troubled by eating sweets (as you will read later sugary foods can cause bloating, diarrhea, and abdominal pain following other types of surgery), and as a result they may consume excessive amounts of sweets. This behavior has been linked to poor long-term weight loss. At ten years this procedure has an 80 percent failure rate (meaning much of the initial weight lost is regained). In addition 15 to 20 percent of people who have this procedure require a reoperation due to blockage of the polypropylene band or reflux of stomach acid into the esophagus. Because of these difficulties, it is unlikely that your doctor will suggest vertical-banded gastroplasty.

What about gastric banding? Is it more successful than vertical-banded gastroplasty?

Gastric banding (Figure 2.2), also known as lap band surgery, uses an inflatable silicone band to divide the stomach and create a very small stomach pouch. While the diameter of the band is generally about two inches (five centimeters), the surgeon can adjust the diameter by pumping saline into the band from a reservoir implanted under the patient's skin. Just as with vertical-banded gastroplasty, blockage of the band can be problematic, and unfortunately the reservoir implanted beneath the skin doesn't last forever. Consequently, weight regain with this method can also occur. In general gastric banding is no more successful than vertical-banded gastroplasty, and it too can result in iron and vitamin B_{12} deficiency.

What about biliopancreatic diversion with duodenal switch (BDDS) procedure? I have heard that you can eat more following a BDDS procedure than after purely restrictive procedures—is this true?

Biliopancreatic diversion with duodenal switch (Figure 2.3) is the classic malabsorptive procedure. It does not dramatically reduce the size of the stomach, yet weight loss can be very significant. In fact, this procedure is used most commonly with people who need the most dramatic weight loss. Since the stomach is not dramatically reduced in size, people can eat more normal amounts following this type of surgery than following restrictive surgery. In the BDDS procedure, food bypasses contact with most of the duodenum and all of the jejunum. Instead, the very beginning of the duodenum (or first part of the small intestine) is connected directly to the ileum (last part of the small intestine), bypassing most of the duodenum and the entire jejunum.

FIGURE 2.3 Biliopancreatic Diversion with Duodenal Switch

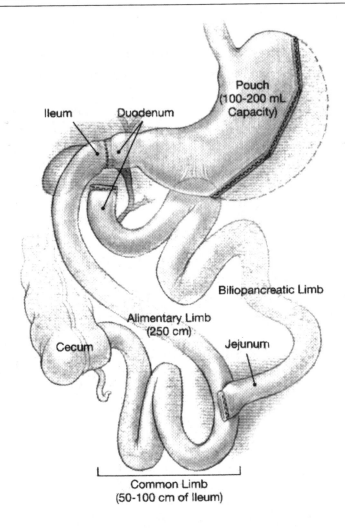

Source: JAMA, December 11, 2002—Vol. 288, No. 22, p. 2794. Illustrated by C. Lynn. Reprinted with permission. Note: 5 mL = 1 teaspoon; 2.54 cm = 1 inch.

The pancreas and gall bladder have ducts that carry digestive juices and enzymes to the duodenum. These enzymes and digestive juices allow for the breakdown of the food we eat. Once food is broken down it can be absorbed in the duodenum and jejunum of the lower intestine. Since this procedure prevents the digestive juices and enzymes in the duodenum and jejunum from making contact with food until almost the end of the ileum (see Figure 2.3), calories from food are simply not absorbed effectively. This allows dramatic weight loss to occur, but it also results in a number of complications.

What are the complications of biliopancreatic diversion with duodenal switch, and how much weight can a person expect to lose?

Because this procedure works by prevention of nutrient absorption, vitamin deficiencies are a common problem. During the year following surgery, 30 percent of people develop anemia, and 30 to 50 percent of people develop a deficiency of the fat-soluble vitamins including vitamins A, D, E, and K. A small number of people (3 to 5 percent) actually develop protein-calorie malnutrition and require hospitalization for intravenous protein replacement. Because the potential for vitamin and mineral deficiencies following this particular surgical procedure is so great, it is crucial for you to maintain regular follow-up with the nurses, doctors, and especially dietitians at your gastric bypass center. Also, because food has limited contact with the intestines diarrhea (due to rapid transit time) and foul-smelling stools (due to incomplete digestion) are a common problem. The good news is that most people lose between 75 to 80 percent of excess weight (this corresponds to about 35 to 45 percent of baseline weight) and maintain the weight loss long-term.

What does the Roux-en-Y procedure entail? Is this the type of surgery that celebrities like Al Roker and Carnie Wilson underwent?

The Roux-en-Y procedure (Figure 2.4) is the most commonly performed bariatric surgery. Reportedly, both Al Roker and Carnie Wilson underwent the Roux-en-Y surgery. While it is primarily restrictive, it does have a malabsorptive component (but nothing like the BDDS). This procedure creates a very small stomach pouch, which is stapled horizontally, separating it from the rest of the stomach. In some cases the small stomach pouch is physically separated from the rest of the stomach. Initially the stomach pouch can hold about one or two tablespoons of food. The small intestine is cut near the beginning of the jejunum (second part of the small intestine), and the long portion of the jejunum is attached to the newly created small stomach. Food travels from the small stomach directly into the jejunum. Digestive juices and bile still enter the duodenum, but these juices do not meet the food until farther downstream (see Figure 2.4). The portion of the intestine containing the digestive juices is reunited with the portion containing food. Since food is in contact with the digestive juices for less than the normal period of time, some malabsorption occurs. Because of its low complication rate and high degree of success, the Roux-en-Y is generally accepted to be the best and safest bariatric procedure.

FIGURE 2.4 Roux-en-Y Gastric Bypass

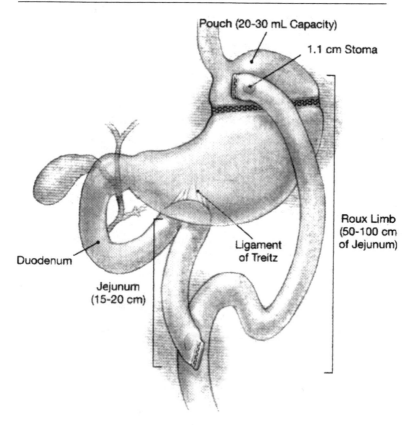

Pouch (20-30 mL Capacity)

1.1 cm Stoma

Roux Limb
(50-100 cm
of Jejunum)

Ligament
of Treitz

Duodenum

Jejunum
(15-20 cm)

Source: JAMA, December 11, 2002—Vol. 288, No. 22, p. 2794. *Illustrated by
C. Lynn. Reprinted with permission. Note: 5 mL = 1 teaspoon; 2.54 cm = 1 inch.*

I have heard people can develop something called the "dumping syndrome" after Roux-en-Y. What is this, and can it be prevented?

Although nausea, bloating, stomach cramps, and diarrhea (known as the dumping syndrome) can occur due to food passing quickly from the small stomach pouch into the jejunum, this is generally not a major problem. The dumping syndrome seems to occur more frequently after a person eats sweets. It is believed that part of the success of the Roux-en-Y procedure is because when people find that eating sweets causes this problem they stop eating them.

When you think of sweets, your first thoughts are probably chocolate, ice cream, and cookies. While these foods can certainly cause the dumping syndrome, potatoes are also frequently implicated. This is because potatoes are a "high glycemic index" food, meaning that potatoes are rapidly digested to sugar (glucose). One of my patients of Irish heritage had practically lived on potatoes, but now he found he couldn't tolerate them in any form. Post–gastric bypass the only thing he longed for was potatoes. "I'm Irish," he said, "they're in my blood." But time is a great healer, and losing 105 pounds helped, too. He has now adjusted to life without potatoes.

What other foods have a high glycemic index and might cause the dumping syndrome?

Foods such as white rice, white bread, some breakfast cereals including high-sugar cereals and, surprisingly, cereals such as cornflakes may also cause dumping syndrome.

Does the dumping syndrome ever go away?

Dr. Bruno Balsiger and his colleagues from the Mayo Clinic in Rochester, Minnesota, have followed a group of about two hundred gastric bypass patients for several years. They discovered that dumping is most prominent during the first postoperative year. Although it never completely goes away, it certainly becomes less of a problem over time.

What amount of weight loss can people expect after undergoing the Roux-en-Y procedure? Is this weight loss maintained long-term?

Weight loss with the Roux-en-Y procedure is quite good, with most people losing between 65 to 75 percent of their excess weight within the first year (this corresponds to about 35 percent of total weight). While some people do gain a considerable amount of weight back over the following three to five years, most do not.

At what point after the surgery will I lose the most weight? Is it slow and steady or quick?

The first six months after the surgery is known as the rapid weight loss phase. Immediately following surgery your stomach will be quite swollen and you simply will not be hungry. At this stage you will be taking in liquids only and your weight will fall dramatically. Many of my patients have lost twenty to thirty pounds during their first postoperative month. As you begin to eat real food weight loss slows a little, but you can expect very steady and substantial weight loss for the first six months. Most people report that they do not feel hungry, even at mealtimes, for up to six months. At about six months many people find that their appetite returns. Nonetheless weight loss generally continues for another six months, but at a slower rate. In general, after about a year, further weight loss becomes more difficult without real effort. By a year most people will have lost about 65 to 75 percent of their excess weight. This means that in order to achieve their ideal body weight they need to continue to lose. Unfortunately, at about a year a person's new stomach will have stretched a bit, making it much easier to consume larger portions. At this point food choices and exercise help determine if a person will achieve his or her ideal body weight.

I met Horace for the first time as he lay in a hospital bed after having an angioplasty (a procedure in which a thin catheter containing an inflatable balloon is used to open a blocked heart artery). I was asked to help manage his cholesterol, blood pressure, and diabetes. As I reviewed his history, it was clear to me that his most significant problem was his weight. There was no weight in his medical chart because he was too heavy for a conventional scale. His best guess was that he weighed somewhere around 350 pounds. At our first meeting I did little more than adjust his medications. I told him that as soon as he got out of the hospital we would call him and arrange a follow-up appointment to discuss diet, exercise, and weight loss. Horace, a widower, lived alone and admitted that convenience foods were his main source of calories. He had no regular exercise program and was nearing retirement. I knew my work was cut out for me.

Initially, by participating in our hospital cardiac rehabilitation program and following the diet we outlined for him, Horace did lose weight. Within six months he was able to be weighed on a conventional scale. His lowest weight, however—296 pounds—was too difficult for him to sustain.

Eight months later he was over 350 pounds again. At that point, we began discussing gastric bypass surgery. I explained to Horace that given his medical conditions (diabetes, heart disease, high blood pressure, high cholesterol, and sleep apnea) and his age (he was now sixty-three), he was at very high risk for complications related to surgery. Nonetheless, I suggested that he attend an informational session on gastric bypass.

Horace didn't take the risk lightly—in fact it took him almost a year to get up the courage to really consider having the procedure. Once he did decide, he was required to lose 15 pounds—and this, too, took quite a bit of time. Finally, after careful consideration, Dr. Paul Kispert at Dartmouth Medical Center performed Horace's surgery.

His rapid recovery surprised everyone involved in his care. He was out of the hospital in three days. Since his surgery he has lost over 100 pounds. He no longer requires drugs for his diabetes or blood pressure. His cholesterol is now being managed with a tiny dose of medication, and his sleep apnea is a thing of the past. He is exercising regularly and he has so much more energy that he has taken a part-time job and is volunteering for his local church several times a week. His only regret, he says, is that it took him so long to make up his mind to undergo the surgery.

CHAPTER THREE

The Risks

What are the risks of the Roux-en-Y procedure?

As with any major surgery, there can be complications. One of the most common in the Roux-en-Y procedure is blood clots in the legs. This occurs in about 0.2 percent of people undergoing the Roux-en-Y procedure. The clots have the potential to travel to the lungs, where they can have serious consequences. In order to prevent this you will be given blood thinners following surgery. You may also be asked to wear compression stockings. These are very tight stockings that have been proven to reduce blood clots in postoperative patients. Your doctor will want you to get up and walk as soon after surgery as possible. No, no one is trying to torture you. Early ambulation has also been proven to reduce the risk of blood clots. Finally, although the risk of blood clots is highest in the days immediately following surgery, if you notice unexplained swelling in your legs or sudden shortness of breath once you are home from the hospital, contact your physician and get yourself evaluated.

Another risk is that occasionally food or liquids will leak out of the stomach instead of traveling directly into the jejunum. While this can be a serious complication occurring in about 1 percent of procedures, it can generally be corrected. If this happens to you, you will need to return to the operating room. In general, one day after your gastric bypass surgery you will go down to the radiology department and drink something called gastrographin (this is a liquid that will show up on an x-ray). After you drink the gastrographin you will have an x-ray to make sure there is no leakage. If there is a problem, it can be addressed immediately.

Is it possible to have a leak that is not identified by the gastrographin x-ray study?

Unfortunately the answer is yes! Sometimes it is difficult to identify a leak. Signs and symptoms of a leak may include rapid heart rate, rapid breathing, left shoulder pain, and anxiety. While these signs and symptoms may seem quite vague, they are not normal and certainly would prompt your doctor to investigate fully.

I have heard that pneumonia is a risk following any weight loss surgery. How do the lungs get involved?

After any abdominal surgery pneumonia is a risk. This is because it hurts to take a deep breath. When a person fails to breathe deeply a portion of the lung may collapse, setting the stage for pneumonia. Approximately 0.1 percent of people undergoing the Roux-en-Y procedure develop pneumonia. Simply breathing deeply following surgery reduces this risk. In order to facilitate deep breathing the hospital staff will teach you to use a handheld plastic device called an incentive spirometer. You will be instructed to inhale deeply with your mouth around the tube attached to the incentive spirometer. The more air you take into your lungs, the more you will move the little ball inside the spirometer. My advice is: use it, even if it hurts a little (or a lot).

Are there any other abdominal organs at risk for being injured during weight loss surgery?

Your doctor will be operating on your stomach and intestine, but there are other organs in the same area. The most important neighboring organ is the spleen, which can be injured. Even in the hands of the best surgeons, this may occur in up to 0.8 percent of people. If the spleen is injured it may need to be removed. While you can live without a spleen, you may be at increased risk for certain infections afterward.

Is there a risk for the incision site becoming infected?

Unfortunately, due to poor circulation or underlying diabetes, many overweight people have difficulty healing wounds. Therefore, it is not surprising that between 1 and

5 percent of people develop wound infections at the site of surgery. The risk of wound infection is greatly reduced if surgery can be performed using a laparoscope (a small instrument with a light on the end). In such a procedure, there are generally six very small incision sites instead of one large one. As a result, hospitalization and recovery time are dramatically reduced.

In general, a person's size and whether or not he or she has had previous abdominal surgery are the deciding factors for determining if the laparoscopic approach can be used. The larger the person the less likely he or she will qualify for laparoscopic surgery. Laparoscopic surgery is much more technically demanding than the traditional procedure, but if you qualify for it, it definitely makes recovery quicker and less painful. Most centers that perform a lot of weight loss procedures will offer this technique. The more laparoscopic procedures a surgeon performs, the better he or she will get at it. I recommend asking your potential surgeon about his or her experience (don't worry about hurting the surgeon's feelings — it is your body).

I am afraid to ask this question, but what are my chances of dying during or immediately following weight loss surgery?

This is obviously the most important question to ask. Death occurs in about 0.5 percent (one in every two hundred) of people who undergo this procedure. While the risk is low, it is not zero. This is about the same risk as any other major abdominal surgery. But this is elective surgery. Making the decision to have bariatric surgery may feel like taking a big risk. You are right, it is a big risk, but there are things you can do to reduce it. For example, quitting smoking, losing some weight (most programs require this), and developing an exercise program (even a little walking) before surgery can reduce your risk of major complications and death following surgery.

How can I rationalize surgically changing my insides and risking significant complications, even death, just to lose weight?

This is a question that nearly every person who is contemplating bariatric surgery asks him- or herself along the way. Many wonder if they are risking their lives in the name of vanity.

An article in the *Journal of the American Medical Association* (January 8, 2003) reported that marked obesity in a man aged twenty to thirty could reduce his life expectancy by up to thirteen years. An extremely obese woman in this same age range might expect to lose up to eight years compared to her normal-weight friends. These are not small numbers. People who are overweight are more likely to develop obesity-related illnesses such as heart disease, pulmonary hypertension, stroke, diabetes, sleep apnea, and arthritis. And obese people are much more likely than lean people to develop blood clots in the legs and lungs, gallstones, pancreatitis, abdominal hernia, fatty liver, polycystic ovary syndrome, high blood pressure, arthritis, gout, lower back pain, infertility, urinary incontinence, and cataracts.

So it is not in the name of vanity that you are considering surgery. Your decision to go in for this operation may literally save your life. Nonetheless, many of these problems may be still very abstract for you. You may feel perfectly well and quite unafflicted by any problems related to your obesity. This is especially likely to be true if you are young. In my experience a person's body is remarkably resilient until around the age of thirty or forty. After forty, the walls start tumbling down. Although there are a few people like my husband's uncle Joe, who lived to be ninety-two even though he was one hundred pounds above his ideal weight for most of his adult life, he was clearly the exception, not the rule.

In the end, bariatric surgery is a bit of a leap of faith. You need to believe that weighing less is likely to make you a healthier, happier person. I can only speak for my patients when I say that each and every one of them has found the benefits of gastric bypass to far exceed any drawbacks. All of my patients who have undergone the procedure have told me they would do it again if necessary. Although most have had a relatively event-free recovery, they all admit that there were many bumps along the road.

What about overall satisfaction? A year after surgery, how do people feel about their decision to have gastric bypass surgery?

My personal experience has been overwhelmingly positive. To date I have not encountered a single person who regrets the decision to undergo gastric bypass surgery. I am however only one physician.

Dr. Bruno Balsiger and colleagues at the Mayo Clinic in Rochester, Minnesota, polled about one hundred patients a full three years after surgery. Ninety-three percent were "very satisfied" with their surgery. Most people reported that even at three years their appetite remained diminished. Although about 10 percent of people reported either constipation or heartburn periodically, only 1 percent reported frequent vomiting. Diarrhea more than once a week was the only common complaint, occurring in about 20 percent of those polled.

When food intolerances were assessed, milk and red meat stood out as the most frequent intolerances, occurring in 23 percent and 14 percent respectively. In the case of milk the intolerance is generally lactose intolerance manifested as abdominal bloating and cramping, whereas with red meat the intolerance is simply an acquired aversion.

I have a friend who had gastric bypass surgery who ended up having not only the gastric bypass but the removal of her gallbladder at the same time. Is this common?

This is very common. Before surgery you will almost certainly undergo an ultrasound of your gallbladder. If you have existing gallstones then your gallbladder will be removed at the time of surgery. The reason this is done is that the rapid weight loss you will experience following gastric bypass can increase the risk of developing symptomatic gallstones. If you already have gallstones the risk is high enough that preventive removal of your gallbladder is warranted.

What if I don't have my gallbladder removed at the time of surgery? What is the chance I will require a second operation due to gallbladder disease?

Because rapid weight loss results in gallstone formation in up to 40 percent of people, many who were not found to have gallstones at the time of surgery will develop them during the first postoperative year. Fortunately only about 15 percent of people will develop symptoms related to gallstones. In general, following surgery the gallbladder is only removed in symptomatic people.

Is there any medication that can help prevent gallstones from forming during rapid weight loss?

One large multicenter study reported that treating patients with ursodiol (a medication that prevents gallstone formation) at a dose of 600 mg per day was highly effective in preventing gallstone formation during the rapid weight loss phase immediately following surgery. In this study gallstones formed in 32 percent of people who received placebo (sugar pill) versus 2 percent of those treated with ursodiol at 600 mg per day. Based on this data some centers routinely use 600 mg of ursodiol per day for about six months following surgery.

There wasn't a diet Megan wouldn't try, but she found that the more she participated in the various commercial weight loss programs and even the trendy ones, the more she thought about food. The results of her many attempts were all the same: some weight loss, though never quite enough, hitting a plateau, and gaining all of the weight back.

About six years ago, Megan and a close friend both began thinking seriously about gastric bypass. Megan researched the procedure and came to the conclusion that it might be the answer to her weight battle. As a nurse, she also recognized that although she hadn't yet had any complications related to her obesity, it was just a matter of time.

Both of Megan's parents were diabetic, and Megan knew that diabetics were at high risk for heart disease and kidney problems and unfortunately, she knew from the sad experience of her mother's death that diabetes could also mean the loss of eyesight and the loss of her life.

After her mother's death, Megan began to again consider gastric bypass. She began by attending several support group meetings. Her father opposed the idea vigorously. Rather than trying to convince him on her own, Megan invited him to come to her support group with her. In the meeting he attended, medical staff first discussed the gastric bypass procedure and statistics, and then people were free to ask questions and make comments. At the conclusion of the meeting Megan's dad's mind was changed. "If you want to do it, you should go for it," Megan's father said to her.

The weight came off very rapidly at first. For the first six months Megan did not feel hungry. In fact she had to remind herself to eat. She has had very few complications, but has required one procedure. About a month after her gastric bypass, Megan suddenly couldn't keep anything down, even water. Via endoscopy, her physicians looked into her stomach pouch and found that she had developed a stricture— a scar impeding any passage of food or liquid out of the pouch into the intestines. Luckily it was easily dilated and has never returned. Nonetheless, it was nerve-racking.

Six months after the surgery, her appetite returned and she has worked hard to eat just three meals a day.

Megan believes that gastric bypass was the best decision for her. But that doesn't preclude regrets. She wishes she could drink fluids with her meals. She would love to occasionally be able to have an ice cream cone—but she can no longer tolerate ice cream. The one time she tried it she vomited. She misses beef and has great difficulty eating chicken. Pasta she finds "just sits" in her stomach, so she avoids it. And she misses the big restaurant meals (appetizer, salad, bread, dinner, and dessert). Of course she acknowledges that those types of meals are what got her into trouble in the first place.

Megan lost eighty pounds and to date has kept it off. She attributes her success to eating three times a day and completely avoiding snacks. Megan also swears by regular attendance to her support group meetings. "I gain a lot from those meetings—they keep me strong. For working through the different issues you face along your journey, support is crucial. The surgery is a powerful tool in what I am sure will be a lifelong journey. It takes time for the mind and body (stomach) to come to a mutually acceptable place where food can finally be used for the purpose for which it was intended—that is, to nourish the body. The support groups help you gain insight into behaviors that may have led to obesity. More importantly they help you remain strong as you go through your personal journey."

She has grown used to having shrimp cocktail as her meal, eating slowly, and enjoying the company of good friends. When asked what was the best advice she got from someone who had already had gastric bypass Megan said, "When you are experimenting with new foods—do it at home." Megan only realized how important this advice was when she tried something new in a restaurant and ended up vomiting.

CHAPTER FOUR

Preparing for Your Surgery

Will I need to have a cardiac stress test (also called an exercise test) before surgery?

It is possible your surgeon will want you to have an exercise stress test prior to your surgery. People who are likely to require a stress test include people who have had heart disease, diabetes, or a stroke. In addition if you have multiple heart disease risk factors including high blood pressure, high cholesterol, cigarette smoking, or a strong family history of heart disease your doctor may request that you have a stress test. Men over the age of forty-five and women over fifty-five may also require a stress test.

There are a number of different options when it comes to stress tests. In the first type of stress test you will have small pads (electrodes) placed on your upper body to monitor your heart rate and rhythm. Once you have the electrodes in place you will be asked to begin walking on a treadmill or pedaling on a stationary bike. In order to get an accurate assessment of your heart health you will be asked to exercise for several minutes. At first, the pace will be slow and easy but it will gradually get a bit more difficult. In order to get the most information possible, you should exercise as long as you can. If you develop chest, arm, or jaw pressure or pain, shortness of breath, leg pain, or dizziness during the test, be sure to let the physician performing the test know. During the stress test your blood pressure, heart rate, and heart rhythm will be monitored. People who experience a dramatic change in blood pressure with exercise may have underlying cardiac problems and may require a more complete cardiac evaluation. Likewise if a person is noted to have changes in his or her electrocardiogram (ECG or EKG) with exercise (indicating that the heart muscle is not getting proper blood flow during exercise), further heart testing may be indicated. While no test is perfect, in general if you do well on a stress test, your surgery will probably go well from a cardiac standpoint. On the other hand, if the stress test indicates possible cardiac problems, these will need to be addressed prior to surgery. This might mean the addition of some new medications. Alternatively it could mean a cardiac procedure (angioplasty or even bypass surgery). The bottom line is that it makes more sense to find out about a problem and correct it before surgery than to go into the operation and get into trouble mid-procedure.

The other thing that an exercise stress test can do for you is give you an "exercise prescription" prior to surgery. In other words your doctor will be able to evaluate your stress test and tell you that it is safe to get your heart rate to a certain level with exercise. This is certainly important because it allows you to feel safer from a cardiac standpoint as you develop an exercise program before and after surgery.

In terms of the nuts and bolts of having this test, make sure you don't eat, drink, smoke, or have any caffeine for three hours before your stress test. Also make sure you wear sneakers or good walking shoes and a two-piece outfit—you will have electrodes on your chest and upper body (women are given a hospital gown to wear, while men typically perform the test topless, although a gown can be requested). The entire test takes about thirty minutes. In preparation for the stress test, you may be instructed to withhold taking certain medications. Make sure to ask the person performing the stress test when you should resume taking the medications you have held.

If I cannot exercise, how will my surgeon assess my cardiac status prior to surgery?

Many overweight people have difficulty completing a regular stress test. But just because you have difficulty walking on a treadmill isn't a reason not to evaluate your heart. In fact, it is probably even more important to evaluate the heart in a person who is out of shape. Surgery does "stress" the heart, and it is crucial to be sure a person's heart will withstand surgery. If this is your situation, one option available to your doctor is a dobutamine stress echocardiogram. In this type of stress test, dobutamine, which is a medication that makes the heart beat faster and stronger, will be infused into your vein. Even though you are not actually exercising, your heart thinks you are. Once you have been injected with the dobutamine, a technician will place an echo machine (transducer) against your chest wall. Ultrasound waves will reflect (echo) off the heart, and the echo machine is able to create a two-dimensional image of your heart and heart valves. This type of test has the ability to assess the size, pumping strength, and function of the heart muscle and valves. If you do have areas of your heart that are not getting enough blood flow because of cholesterol blockages in the heart (coronary) arteries the results of this test are likely to be abnormal.

Just as in a standard stress test, you will have electrodes placed on your chest and again, you will want to wear a two-piece outfit. When scheduling this test, make sure you ask if you should hold any of your usual medications prior to the study. In general, beta-blockers are not taken prior to the test and many diabetic medications are also held. Some doctors ask you to hold calcium channel blockers too. When you arrive for the test an intravenous line (IV) will be inserted into your arm to deliver the dobutamine, and electrodes will be placed on your chest. The dose of dobutamine will gradually be increased as the test goes on. Some people experience side effects from the dobutamine. If you experience tremors, nausea, or headache be sure to let the technician know.

Every once in a while a person does not get an acceptable increase in his or her heart rate with dobutamine. In such a case, atropine may be given. Since atropine can cause problems in people with glaucoma or in people who have trouble urinating (generally due to an enlarged prostate gland), be sure to alert the technician if you have either of these problems. This test will take longer than a standard stress test. Be prepared to spend at least two hours at your doctor's office for the dobutamine stress echocardiogram.

Still another option for people who have difficulty exercising is a persantine sestamibi stress test. Like dobutamine, persantine is a drug that mimics exercise. When injected into a person's vein, persantine makes the heart beat faster and more forcefully. Sestamibi is nuclear imaging that highlights the heart muscle and allows the physician to evaluate the adequacy of its blood supply. Just as in the dobutamine stress echocardiogram described above, you will probably be instructed to hold certain medications the day of the test.

Your heart will be evaluated with persantine in your system (mimicking exercise) and at rest. The evaluation will include both electrocardiograms and pictures. This stress test takes about three hours to complete.

I was told I needed to lose fifteen pounds before I could be scheduled for a gastric bypass procedure. I am seeking this procedure because I have been unable to lose weight with traditional diets. Why do I need to go on a diet so that I can have a weight loss surgery? Is the team at my gastric bypass center just trying to discourage me? This does not seem fair.

You're right! At first this seems totally unfair. It seems that it maybe even defeats the purpose of considering the procedure. And it really does make preparation for the procedure hard work. That being said, there are a number of reasons that your surgeon may require weight loss, and not one of them is to discourage you. Most important, weight loss prior to surgery can diminish your abdominal fat and make it much easier for your surgeon to see your internal organs and perform your surgery safely. It is also true that losing weight (our center generally requires weight loss equaling

8 percent of a person's body weight) demonstrates a commitment to the program. If you are successful at losing a small amount of weight preoperatively, you are likely to do well postoperatively when you are only able to consume tiny amounts of food at any given time. In fact, during the first few days after surgery you will only be allowed water, and for between two and six weeks you will only consume liquids. So even if your doctor seems to be asking you to lose what seems like an inordinate amount of weight, it is likely to make your postoperative course much smoother. While I know this explanation doesn't make the weight loss easier, at least it gives you the rationale behind the requirement.

In addition to asking me to lose weight prior to surgery, my doctor has asked me to quit smoking. I don't think I can lose weight and quit smoking.

Once again your doctor is not trying to sabotage your surgery. People who smoke do not do as well following any surgery requiring general anesthesia as nonsmokers. If you are a smoker it is likely that it will be more difficult to get you to breathe on your own following surgery than if you were a nonsmoker. Quitting even for a short period of time prior to surgery can make coming off the respirator easier. Quitting smoking on top of losing weight may seem like a major task, but you will be in much better shape for surgery if you do. If you remain off cigarettes long-term following surgery you will dramatically reduce your risk of heart disease, lung disease, and many forms of cancer. A smoke-free you, a lighter you, a healthier you. Think of how you can really change your life in the next six to twelve months.

For some people a smoking cessation aid makes quitting a lot easier. One way to help determine if you might benefit from a smoking cessation tool is to answer one simple question from the Fagerström Nicotine Dependency Assessment. Do you smoke within thirty minutes of getting up in the morning? Studies have shown that smokers who "need" that first morning cigarette are the most highly addicted people. If this is your situation, you can still become a nonsmoker, but it will be more difficult for you than a person who can wait until noon for a cigarette, and a smoking cessation aid such as Wellbutrin or nicotine replacement may be very helpful.

Why do I need to have a psychological evaluation prior to this procedure?

While most people who discuss bariatric surgery with their physician have an essentially normal psychological makeup, a small but significant minority have serious psychological issues. While most of these psychological issues do not preclude undergoing gastric bypass surgery, they do need to be addressed. Sometimes the psychological problems can be treated prior to surgery. However, some issues will require therapy long after bypass surgery.

Depending on what study you read, anywhere from 19 percent to 28 percent of people who request an evaluation for bariatric surgery will have had a history of major depression. A history of major depression should not exclude you if you otherwise qualify for gastric bypass surgery. However, if you are *presently* very depressed, you should be treated before gastric bypass is performed.

It appears that certain people seeking gastric bypass are more likely to be depressed than others. People at greatest risk appear to be women and persons with binge eating disorder (BED) (see question on binge eating in Chapter One).

Why do you think obese women are at greater risk of being depressed than obese men?

The answer to this question is not clear. From my point of view it is remarkable that most obese people are completely psychologically intact. Obese people face prejudice and discrimination from an early age. Even at the tender age of six, children already harbor prejudice against overweight children. When asked to describe the silhouette of an overweight child, words such as "lazy," "stupid," "ugly," and "cheats" were used.

During adolescence, overweight girls are more commonly teased about their weight than overweight boys. Obese men and women often face prejudice at work, with many employers reporting reluctance or refusal to hire obese people. This bias against the obese appears to be directed more against women than men. As compared to their leaner friends, overweight men and women are less likely to marry. One study found that when compared to leaner women of comparable intelligence, overweight women completed fewer years of school and were less successful in their careers. There is clearly evidence of discrimination against overweight students at the college level. One study found that even with similar qualifications, obese students were less likely to be accepted into respected colleges as compared to leaner ones.

It certainly appears that obese men and women face similar types of discrimination. However, in our society, pressure to have the "perfect body" is much more intense for women than men. While likely only part of the answer, this may explain the higher rate of depression in obese women as compared to men.

I have a history of sexual abuse. I believe my significant weight gain was brought on by the trauma of these events and even think that I subconsciously wanted to be obese to avoid the possibility of intimate relationships. How will I deal with losing weight and becoming more attractive to the opposite sex?

This is a very serious question. What I can do is give you some background that will perhaps surprise you and maybe make you feel less alone. I can't, however, solve this issue for you. A history of sexual abuse should not preclude bariatric surgery, but if this is your situation, you will probably benefit from psychological counseling both before and after your surgery.

It might surprise you to learn that one study found that one-quarter (25 percent) of women seeking treatment for extreme obesity reported a history of childhood sexual abuse. Only 6 percent of a normal-weight control group reported such abuse. What is not clear is whether the abuse leads to overeating (as it seems to have done in your case) or if certain people feel that it is more acceptable to abuse an overweight child or adolescent than his or her normal-weight brothers or sisters. And the abuse doesn't necessarily seem to stop in adolescence. Many obese women report being the victim of sexual abuse.

These statistics are alarming. They are enough to make anyone very angry. They also might help to make you feel less alone. Knowing that you are not alone might help you to open up to your physician or counselor. Given that roughly one-quarter of obese women (the statistics are not as widely available for men) seeking bariatric surgery have experienced unwanted sexual advances and even rape, your doctor should have some experience in dealing with this issue. If your doctor doesn't have experience he or she will surely be able to refer you to a counselor who does. Getting help will allow you to enjoy your new body without fear of unwanted sexual advances in the future. Learning to accept yourself may also make it possible for you to enjoy your intimate relationships more fully.

My entire family is fat—I have a BMI of 42 and I am one of the smallest in my family. Everyone thinks I am crazy to even consider gastric bypass surgery. I love my family and I don't want to be an outcast at family gatherings. On the other hand, I want to live to see my grandchildren and I am afraid I won't. I am forty-four years old and already have diabetes, high blood pressure, and high cholesterol. How can I convince my family that I need this surgery?

You raise an issue that many people seeking bariatric surgery raise. It sounds like you already have a number of consequences related to your weight. It might help to let your family know that, statistically speaking, by having the surgery you have a greater than 90 percent chance of controlling your diabetes, blood pressure, and cholesterol without medications.

Obesity contributes to about 300,000 deaths in the United States per year, and it costs the health-care system about 117 billion dollars annually. I mentioned earlier in this book that a recent article in the *Journal of the American Medical Association* (January 8, 2003) found that marked obesity in a man aged twenty to thirty could reduce his life expectancy by up to thirteen years. An extremely obese woman in this same age range might expect to lose up to eight years compared to her normal-weight friends. People who are overweight are more likely to develop obesity-related illnesses such as heart disease, pulmonary hypertension, stroke, diabetes, sleep apnea, and arthritis. And obese people are much more likely than lean people to develop blood clots in the legs and lungs, gallstones, pancreatitis, abdominal hernia, fatty liver, polycystic ovary syndrome, high blood pressure, arthritis, gout, lower back pain, infertility, urinary incontinence, and cataracts.

These are the facts, but knowing something intellectually is one thing—what we feel is another. Chances are your family members who are discouraging you from pursuing gastric bypass surgery are conflicted in their own feelings. They may be afraid that you will die with this surgery. It may seem like a very drastic step to them. Remember back to how you felt when you first began exploring bariatric surgery. You are probably now much better informed than they are. Ask your family members to read this book. Ask them to come to an information seminar at your local hospital. Ask them to attend a support group meeting. These meetings are comforting because you hear from people who have had the procedure. They will tell you the truth about the ups and downs. Maybe you will even convince someone in your family to explore gastric bypass as well.

The above comments give your family members the benefit of the doubt and assume that their concerns are all related to fear for your health. We all (no matter how thin or overweight) have a darker side. Some of your friends and family will be conflicted. Yes, they will be worried about the risk of surgery, but they will also be concerned that you are going to suddenly get thin and won't want to be with them anymore. This is especially true of spouses and significant others. Other family members may be afraid that you will suddenly look much better than they do. Others might be jealous of all the attention you will get as you are rapidly losing weight.

If you suspect that your spouse or significant other may feel threatened by the new you, you need to deal with this now. Some obese people have difficult personal relationships. If you have endured years of taunting by your partner (about your obesity) but put up with it for whatever reason, you will have a lot of baggage to get through. It is true that sometimes following major weight loss women and men who have been in difficult or abusive relationships finally have the courage to end them. There are some relationships that might not be salvageable. It is as important for you to understand how your spouse, significant other, or family members are feeling as it is for them to understand you. They are very much a part of your surgery, but you are getting all the attention. It is crucial for you to affirm your love for your spouse and family as you become thinner. This is especially true if your partner is also overweight. You need to make sure your partner knows that even though you are thinner and healthier you still find him or her attractive and desirable.

As you become thinner you will need to develop a regular exercise program. Your spouse, significant other, and family members may not exercise. Since you will be starting out slowly this might be a way for your family members and loved ones to join you and become fitter themselves. Developing a daily walking program will help you lose weight and keep it off and is a nonthreatening form of exercise for your family to try. In fact it has been my experience that the people who are most successful with long-term weight loss following bariatric surgery are those people who exercise daily. (More on developing an exercise program later — see the question, "How will exercise help me before surgery?" later in this chapter, as well as Chapter Seven.)

As you work through the issues surrounding the new thinner you, you and your family may benefit from some counseling. In the end, the people who really love you will stick with you and be supportive. It may take some people a little longer than others to accept the new you. For many it is not because they don't love you, it is because of their insecurity surrounding their own bodies. Remember to be patient.

I am going in for my gastric bypass procedure next week. What should I take in my suitcase?

I have polled my patients regarding this issue. In general what you should pack is obvious, but there may be some things you haven't thought of.

- A couple of loose-fitting nightgowns or pajamas — since you will be hooked up to an intravenous line you may choose to use the hospital gowns. By the time you are ready for your own nightclothes you may be about to go home. However many people prefer their own clothes as they are certainly more modest. Remember you can always wear two gowns — one in the front and another like a robe — this way everything is covered.

- Socks and slippers.

- Toiletries. Toothbrush and toothpaste (don't depend on the hospital for these, they are generally of poor quality), deodorant, your own soap (will generally smell better than the hospital brand), hairbrush, and comb. Women, if you wear makeup regularly bring it and use it — it will lift your spirits. Men who shave regularly should bring their razor and shaving cream for the same reason. Shampoo and conditioner (as soon as you can take a shower do so, and wash your hair — this will make you feel better). Body lotion and lip balm (the hospital air can be quite dry and these will help). With regard to the lip balm — choose a flavored brand — one of my patients told me it felt like a snack.

- Bath powder. Some hospital mattresses are covered in plastic — this can make your back and buttocks sweaty as you sit in bed. Powder will help keep you feeling better. This is probably available in the little sack of toiletries issued by the hospital, but don't count on it — bring your own.

- Many of my patients have told me that their hospital room was too hot or too cold. You can't bring a heater, but you can bring a mini fan and I suggest that you do.

- Bring this book and a novel. Since it will hurt to laugh, the novel shouldn't be excessively funny.

- A pillow. Most people like to use their own pillow. Since you will be having major abdominal surgery it will be uncomfortable to cough or laugh. Holding your pillow up to your chest when you need to cough or laugh decreases the discomfort. I suggest a brightly colored pillowcase — it will cheer you up.

- Some people bring a camera to take a photo imme-diately before surgery. I recommend either taking the photo on the morning of surgery before leaving your home or at the hospital. You will want to take follow-up photos at least once a month. Some people pick out an outfit and put it on once a month for a snapshot. If you do this also take a photo of yourself in something that fits once a month so your new body can be seen.

- Very loose clothes to go home in — women may choose a very loose dress, men should choose a very loose sweat suit.

- Music can be very soothing both before and after surgery. Some people bring a little boom box, others bring a little tape or CD player with earphones.

- Photos of your friends, family, or favorite place can be calming as well.

What should I do before my surgery to prepare my home for my recovery?

When you first arrive home you will feel sore and somewhat weak. You want to make things as easy on yourself as you can. To answer this question I have once again polled my patients for their ideas. I also have added some of my own more medically oriented suggestions.

- You won't need much food, but you will want to stock up on all the items listed in the Stage 1 and Stage 2 diets (see Chapter Six).

- If you don't have a recliner you may want to borrow one or rent one from a furniture rental store. Some people find it difficult to get to their bedroom, especially if it is on the second floor. Some find lying totally flat initially uncomfortable and find a recliner a much better choice. It is also easier to get up from a recliner than a bed.

- If you do manage to sleep in your own bed following surgery it is nice to have a full body pillow.

- A shower seat and a raised seat for the toilet make your trips to the bathroom much easier.

- Prior to going in to the hospital try to take care of as many little life details as possible: return movies and library books, pay your bills, clean the house, water the plants, send your pet to the kennel for about a week—unless you have someone who can take care of the pet and you feel you will enjoy (maybe even need) the pet's company. Make sure you have at least a three-week supply of all your medications.

- Make sure you leave the hospital with a prescription for pain medication; it is very likely you will need this for at least a few weeks. If possible get the prescription a day or so in advance and send a friend or family member to pick this up. This way the medicine will be waiting for you at home when you arrive.

- If you are a smoker—clear out all your ashtrays and rid your house of cigarettes. It may sound strange, but this is the perfect time to quit. You won't feel like driving to the store to get cigarettes and you will be taking pain medications, which may decrease your cravings for cigarettes. Obviously I don't generally prescribe pain medications for smoking cessation, but you should take advantage of this opportunity. Imagine a thinner nonsmoking you— you will be so much healthier.

- Buy a few new nightgowns or loose-fitting pajamas.

- Buy some soothing music to listen to while you are recovering.

- Buy a few novels—you can only watch so much television.

- If you live alone and have no one to help you at home you really should consider asking your doctor if you are eligible for a few days in a rehabilitation facility. In my hospital we have a rehabilitation unit on location. Alternatively, you might arrange for a daily visit from a home health aide.

- You will probably be sent home with an incentive spirometer—the same plastic breathing device you used in the hospital. Make sure to use it three to four times an hour. This will help keep your airways open and prevent collapse of your air passages, a risk factor for developing pneumonia.

- Since the average person having a gastric bypass is a woman in her thirties or forties, you may have children. Although you will probably want your children around, you will need help caring for them. You might be a single mother or your spouse might need to work during the day. Consider hiring a babysitter or enlisting a friend or family member to help with child care.

- If you can afford to pamper yourself a little, hire someone to come in and clean your house and run errands for the next month (including grocery shopping for the rest of your family—you might not feel like looking at all the foods you cannot eat). Although you may well be back to work in two weeks you will be quite tired by the end of the day and probably will not feel up to additional responsibilities.

I have heard that gastric bypass may increase my chances of getting pregnant. I have been told that the reason I have had so much difficulty in getting pregnant is that I have polycystic ovary syndrome (PCO syndrome). What exactly is PCO syndrome, and is it really true that gastric bypass can cure this?

Polycystic ovary syndrome is a condition in which women fail to ovulate regularly. Some women with PCO syndrome fail to ovulate at all. Most women with PCO syndrome get their first period at about the same time as their peers, but they never become regular. Some women with PCO syndrome stop getting their menstrual period altogether; others have very irregular bleeding. Obese women tend to make an excessive amount of androgens in their adrenal glands (these are small glands that sit on top of the kidneys). Androgens are male hormones. The androgens are responsible for excessive hair growth (on the arms, face, legs, and sometimes chest) that some women with PCO syndrome experience. Much of the excess androgen is converted to estrogen by the fat cells. Ultimately the excess estrogen confuses the pituitary and hypothalamus (two centers in the brain that regulate hormone production) and leads to enlarged ovaries, each with many cysts. The ovaries cease to function properly and infertility results. The good news is that weight loss is by far the best treatment for PCO syndrome. Our bodies are amazingly resilient. One study at the University of Toronto found that following weight loss surgery, 100 percent of women who attempted to become pregnant were successful. Not only were these women successful, their pregnancies were without complications. This is amazing because had they become pregnant when they were still obese, they would have been at high risk for diabetes, high blood pressure, blood clots in the legs, and many other complications throughout the pregnancy. In addition, babies born to obese women are themselves at risk for a number of birth defects and macrosomia (being born oversized).

How will exercise help me before surgery?

Exercise is crucial to your success. But if you have never exercised before in your life, take it slow. As you lose weight, you may find that you actually enjoy exercising and the feeling of pride that comes when your body begins to do what you want it to. In terms of long-term success, diet helps you lose weight while exercise helps you keep it off.

Exercise may be very difficult for you prior to surgery. Your excess weight may cause significant fatigue with exertion as well as causing back or knee problems. Nonetheless, any exercise prior to surgery will probably improve your overall fitness and will likely reduce your recovery time. Before surgery I suggest you discuss exercise with your doctor. He or she may want you to undergo a cardiac stress test (exercise test) (see discussion of stress tests earlier in this chapter) to ensure that you are not at risk for heart trouble with exercise.

If you have never exercised before, or haven't exercised in years, I recommend starting with a walking program prior to surgery. This doesn't need to be formal to begin with. Something as simple as parking your car at the far end of a parking lot and walking in to the store or work will give you some exercise. If this goes well, try walking for five minutes at a time. Over a period of about a month work yourself up to three five-minute walks a day. If all is going well, keep increasing—work up gradually to ten minutes three times a day.

It might be good to walk before each meal. People frequently find that immediately following exercise appetite decreases slightly. If you are truly limited in your ability to walk due to back or knee pain, I recommend water walking. Many pools allow this, and some even have a special walking pool (generally these pools are three feet deep). If you find it embarrassing to get into a bathing suit due to your weight, this might be a problem. Often a pool will be less crowded at a certain time of day. If you can go at that time it might be easier on you. The buoyancy water creates means you are less likely to injure yourself while walking. Swimming is also a great choice. Once again, as with any other exercise program start slow and gradually work up.

Len was always the largest kid in the class. The youngest of five children, he still managed to be the biggest. Len loves everything about food. When he wasn't eating, he was cooking. "It was my hobby," he explains. By his freshman year of high school, Len weighed 200 pounds, a figure he eventually more than doubled into his adulthood. At six feet, four inches, Len's peak was 410 pounds.

Some overweight people have difficulty understanding why they weigh so much more than their friends, believing that they don't actually eat that much. But not Len! He loved to eat, loved "diving in," as he puts it. "I had a huge capacity for volume," he admits.

In spite of his cheerful attitude, however, Len's weight did bother him. He frequently tried to lose weight—and limited success was not difficult. It was nothing for him to shed 50 pounds, but he would soon get bored with whatever diet he was on, and the weight would come right back. After regaining all of the 140 pounds he managed to lose in 1989, Len stopped really trying to lose weight.

His weight was taking its toll. After thirty years as a barber and real estate developer, Len was forced to retire on disability. He underwent a knee replacement, and his back had been badly injured in a fall. He also had difficultly controlling his high blood pressure. At fifty and on disability, Len's future looked bleak.

With his medical problems mounting, he was certain things would only get worse. As it was, he couldn't even walk down the aisles of the supermarket without having to stop due to back pain. And he knew that if he developed a stroke or other serious illness, his wife would not be able to care for him because of his size. He did not want to end up in a nursing home. He knew he was going to have to do something about his weight.

After Len heard about his niece's astonishing success with gastric bypass, Len began to wonder if such an operation might work for him.

Because the surgery was likely to dramatically improve both his cholesterol profile and his blood pressure, the procedure could actually be seen as lifesaving and therefore covered by insurance. And although it wouldn't correct his back or knee troubles, the weight loss associated with the surgery might prevent them from getting any worse.

Len had no problems with his psychiatric evaluation, and his gallbladder study went well. His sleep apnea study, however, indicated that he had sleep apnea (see Chapter Five) and needed to be fitted for a C-PAP machine, which improved the quality of his sleep. Finally, his stress test revealed that he might have previously had a heart attack. This knowledge made the surgery even more important. The weight loss requirement was not a problem for Len as he found weight loss pretty easy—it was the keeping off part that had been hard.

Even though Len understood all the risks associated with surgery, he was not very nervous. He understood that up to one out of every two hundred people who have this surgery die, but he felt confident that he would not be one of them.

Other than eight hours of mild pain requiring pain medication, Len felt great after the surgery. He was a little nervous about taking that first postoperative walk (see first question in Chapter Three). As it turned out, the worst thing about Len's gastric bypass came on day two, when he had to swallow gastrographin. This is a "horrible-tasting" liquid that shows up on x-ray and helps determine if the surgery has been successful. If the gastrographin remains in the new stomach pouch when the person swallows, it is highly unlikely that there will be any problem with food leaking out. Len's study indicated that his surgery had been a success. It was only then that Len was allowed his first sips of water—an experience he described later as "better than drinking champagne."

Len then progressed smoothly from clear liquids to "real food." He very quickly learned which foods were going to cause trouble and which were not. Len has had to swear off some of his favorite foods including homemade pea soup, beef, and pasta with sauce, all of which caused significant vomiting. He also had quite a bit of difficulty with the required protein drinks. And while he used to love tuna and turkey, he now finds he can do without either.

When asked if he has had any regrets, Len admits that he misses his ability to eat. "Going out to dinner will never be the same, and mentally it's hard to accept that I will never be able to eat the way I used to—I mean I'm the guy who used to count on eating my own meal and half of my wife's every time we dined out. Now two months after surgery and over 40 pounds lighter, I know this is permanent. There is no going back. Part of me would like to be able to turn it off and go out to eat the way I used to—maybe just once a month."

Although Len acknowledges that some days are harder than others, he certainly does not regret having gastric bypass surgery. He misses food. But he likes being leaner, he likes moving around more easily, he likes saving money on groceries, and he is learning to cook for two (actually one and a half).

CHAPTER FIVE

Postoperative Concerns and Healing

Tell me about what I can expect when I wake up after the Roux-en-Y procedure. Will I have tubes and drains in all my orifices?

When you wake up it is a strong possibility that you will have a nasogastric tube in place. This tube extends from your nose into your stomach and can help prevent vomiting. This tube may stay in place for a couple of days. Some people will also have a breathing tube. This tube is connected to a respirator and breathes for you while you are under general anesthesia. This is usually removed when you are conscious enough to breathe on your own. A small group of people (generally people with underlying lung disease) have trouble being "weaned" off the respirator and may have the breathing tube in a little longer. Everyone will have a tube draining the abdomen. This removes any excess fluid from the surgical site. Finally most people will also have a tube (catheter) in their bladder, which allows your surgical team to know how much urine you are making while in surgery. It is generally removed soon after the anesthesia wears off. In addition to the tubes and drains you will be wearing something called compression stockings. These are very tight stockings that help prevent blood clots from forming in your legs.

What sort of medications can I expect to receive while in the hospital?

Because gastric bypass puts you at risk for infection, your doctor will most likely order prophylactic (preventive) antibiotics. This preventive measure may save you from developing pneumonia or a wound infection. You will also be treated with blood thinners to prevent blood clots. Most people are also given medicines to prevent ulcer formation and to decrease the risk of developing nausea. You will be given pain medication. This medication is crucial. You want enough to prevent pain but not so much that you fail to breathe deeply or are too groggy to get up and walk. Finally, as mentioned earlier some centers will ask patients to initiate ursodiol aimed at the prevention of gallstones.

I have sleep apnea and use a continuous positive airway pressure (C-PAP) machine. Will I use this following surgery?

In general, people with sleep apnea will be managed without their C-PAP machine for at least a few days. The concern is that the increase in airway pressure these machines create may risk the integrity of the surgical site. In other words the new stomach pouch might fill with air at high pressure — clearly undesirable. I do know that some centers continue to use C-PAP immediately following the gastric bypass procedure. These centers monitor patients very closely for any problems related to the use of C-PAP.

Sleep apnea is a disorder that primarily affects overweight people. The definition of sleep apnea is complete cessation of airflow at the nose and mouth multiple times an hour during sleep. For many people apnea is noted by their bed partners. Some people find out that they have sleep apnea as part of the workup for gastric bypass surgery. In our center sleep studies are performed on most people prior to surgery. We generally want people to be treated with a C-PAP machine for at least two months prior to surgery. A C-PAP machine prevents apnea by increasing airway pressure with each breath a person takes. The C-PAP machine overcomes the tendency of the airway to collapse due to the fatty deposits in the neck or airway tissues. For many people weight loss totally cures their sleep apnea. Consequently, C-PAP may not be required long-term following gastric bypass surgery.

What are my limitations in the first weeks after surgery?

Your surgeon will definitely restrict you from driving for at least one to two weeks following surgery. Obviously if you are still taking pain medication at the two-week mark you should avoid driving until you no longer require it. In addition you will be counseled not to lift any object over five pounds for a couple of weeks. This means no grocery shopping.

How long can I expect to be in the hospital? And how long should I plan to be out of work?

Most people remain in the hospital for anywhere from two to five days. If you do not have someone at home who is able to assist you during your first couple of postoperative weeks, you may find that being discharged to a rehabilitation center is worthwhile. Most people who undergo a laparoscopic Roux-en-Y procedure are back to work in two to three weeks. People who have an open procedure (large mid-abdomen incision) may experience a longer recovery time. Some people do not return to work for a full eight weeks. Everyone is different. You don't know how you will do until you have had the procedure. Try to be flexible and patient with yourself. Obviously for some people eight weeks away from work might present a financial hardship. Some jobs work on an "earned time" system. In this case you would likely be expected to use your earned time (which includes vacation and sick days) to cover your time away from work. If you have a short-term disability policy it is possible that it might kick in.

What kinds of complications can occur in the first few months after the surgery?

One of the big risks associated with gastric bypass surgery, especially if it is performed in the summer, is dehydration.

The stomach pouch is very small, generally one to two ounces. If it is very hot you might have a hard time drinking enough water to prevent dehydration. I advise trying to sip water all day long and staying out of the hot sun.

Vomiting is a very common occurrence. Vomiting can occur early on as a result of swelling (due to the surgery) of the tissue surrounding the opening (stoma) between your new stomach pouch and the intestines. This typically resolves as the swelling due to surgery subsides. But sometimes scar tissue can develop at the same site. If or when the scar tissue creates a physical barrier that food cannot bypass, vomiting occurs. In this situation your surgeon may have to pass an endoscope (a tube with a light on the end that allows your doctor to see into your new pouch and even operate) into your stomach pouch and enlarge the opening a little. Sometimes once solid food is allowed, a person swallows a large piece of meat or other food. The food may have difficulty passing through the stoma. In general, over time the food will pass, but there have been cases where a big piece of meat has had to be removed using an endoscope.

So far we have talked about mechanical obstruction leading to nausea, cramping, and vomiting. In addition to obstruction of the stoma, nausea and vomiting can occur with specific foods. Everyone is different. Some people consistently report vomiting with potatoes. Others find certain fruits and vegetables don't stay down. Still others are primarily troubled by high-fat foods. Some unfortunate people not only get diarrhea (dumping syndrome) with sugary foods, they vomit as well. For many people it is necessary to do some (sometimes painful) experimentation to determine what they can and cannot successfully eat. I do have a few patients who even up to a year following their surgery still experience vomiting a few times a week. However, for most people, the vomiting does not occur regularly after about six months. Many people have to accept that they can no longer eat certain foods they once loved.

Some people develop stomach ulcers or gastritis (irritation of the cells that line the stomach). This occurs in about 2 percent of people who have undergone the Roux-en-Y procedure (it is much more common in people who have undergone gastric banding). Stomach ulcers are generally responsive to medications and rarely require surgical correction.

Another potential late complication of gastric bypass surgery is a hernia. This does not generally happen if a person has had a laparoscopic procedure. A hernia is really a tear in an abdominal muscle with a loop of bowel (intestine) poking through. It is most likely to occur following a surgical procedure that involves a large abdominal incision. We worry about hernias because sometimes the intestine gets stuck outside the abdominal muscle. In such a case the loop of bowel gets cut off from its blood supply and can literally die. In general, if you have a hernia you can see or feel it. Sometimes an incisional hernia will require corrective surgery, or sometimes your surgeon will opt to just follow it closely.

Vitamin deficiencies can develop following any gastric bypass procedure. This is very unlikely to occur if you take supplemental iron, vitamin B_{12}, calcium, vitamin D, and a multivitamin. Vitamin D is most important for people who live in areas like New England and the upper Midwest where winters are long and sunlight scarce. People in warmer areas can get out in the sunlight during the winter and can make their own vitamin D. The dietitian you work

with is likely to recommend specific amounts of these supplements and perhaps a particular brand found in your area
of the country.

**I have one child but had a great deal of difficulty
during my pregnancy with diabetes. If I become
pregnant following surgery, is it likely my pregnancy will be less complicated?**

Yes. Dr. Alan Wittgrove and his colleagues at Alvarado
Hospital and Medical Center in San Diego, California, pub-
lished data in an article in the journal *Obesity Surgery*. They
looked at their database to find women who had had pregnancies both before and after undergoing a gastric bypass
procedure. Overall, pregnancies were much more complicated before gastric bypass surgery than they were after.
The pregnancies in obese women prior to gastric bypass had
been much more frequently complicated by preterm labor,
high blood pressure, and diabetes. When these same women
became pregnant following a successful gastric bypass procedure these complications almost never occurred.

Although Dr. Wittgrove and his colleagues feel pregnancy following gastric bypass is probably lower risk than
before such surgery, they feel it is crucial for regular communication between the bariatric surgeon and the obstetrician to occur.

**If I become pregnant following gastric bypass sur-
gery, will I require any special care throughout my
pregnancy?**

Although special care is generally not necessary, as noted above there should be regular communication between your surgeon and obstetrician throughout your pregnancy. And women who have had a gastric bypass prior to becoming pregnant should be advised that they should not get into the habit of snacking during pregnancy. Continuing with a high protein, low carbohydrate diet is generally recommended. Likewise it is probably not necessary to test these women for gestational diabetes (pregnancy-induced diabetes) with a sugar load at week 28 of pregnancy. Doing so might cause the dumping syndrome (see Chapter Two). In general the standard recommendation is to check blood sugar in the fasting state and two hours after a meal. Finally, women who have had a gastric bypass require iron, vitamin B_{12}, and a multivitamin. These should continue throughout pregnancy, and the prenatal vitamins should be added.

I imagine my doctor will want me to wait a period of time after having gastric bypass before attempting to get pregnant. I am thirty-five years old and feel my biological clock ticking. How long will I have to wait to attempt to become pregnant?

This is a very good question, and you are absolutely correct. Surgeons who perform gastric bypass do generally suggest waiting a full year before trying to become pregnant. During that first year you will be losing weight very quickly. Simply put, babies take a lot of energy and nutrients to produce. You can't be making a baby while losing weight rapidly. Generally you will have reached a stable weight a year after your surgery and you will have ironed out your

nutrient requirements and will be on stable doses of vitamins and other supplements. As noted above, even though
you will require special attention during your pregnancy,
the risks associated with pregnancy one year after gastric
bypass surgery are probably much lower than if you had
conceived before surgery. If this is your situation, I wish you
a nausea-free pregnancy and a quick and painless delivery.
(Having three children, I know the painless part is totally
wishful thinking!)

**I have heard some people say that after a year, it is
very difficult to lose any additional weight. In fact,
many people have told me that some people begin
to gain weight back after about a year. If I go
through this surgery I never want to be obese again.
How can I make the most of the time when weight
loss will be relatively easy, and how can I prevent
weight gain?**

During the first few months following surgery your weight
loss will indeed be at its most rapid. For the first ten to
twelve weeks immediately following surgery your maximum
daily caloric intake will be about 1,000 calories, so of course
you are going to lose weight rapidly. Make sure you don't
eat extra calories during this time period. You can avoid this
by not drinking juices and high-calorie liquids between
meals during the pureed/soft food and real food stages. For
some reason we tend to treat liquid calories differently than
"real food" calories. I suggest that you limit your liquid calories to four ounces of juice per day. Stick with water, herbal
teas, and a limited amount of caffeinated beverages.

A daily exercise program is crucial. While it may be difficult to begin a vigorous exercise program until you have lost some of your excess weight, nonetheless you should work at becoming fitter well before surgery. There is little doubt that daily exercise is one of the most powerful predictors of long-term success at weight maintenance. Even though no one exercise session will burn a tremendous number of calories, exercise seems to increase overall metabolic rate. In other words, people who exercise regularly tend to burn more calories than do their sedentary friends, even when sitting still! Your ultimate goal should be to walk about forty-five to sixty minutes a day.

Finally, don't eat to the point of discomfort. Once you have recovered from surgery you will find that gradually you are able to consume more food at a single sitting than you were right after the operation. Immediately following surgery the new stomach pouch and the stoma (the outlet from the stomach to the small intestine) are swollen and physically prevent you from overeating. But once the swelling has subsided, it is possible to eat a bit more. And over time, the new stomach actually stretches a little. While it will never be the size of your old stomach, some people learn that if they eat a little bit all day long they don't feel uncomfortably full.

Obviously, this defeats the purpose of the surgery! Even with a tiny stomach it is possible to eat enough to gain weight. And in fact most people *do* gain a small amount of weight during the second year following surgery. But you can be different—and being aware of the possibility of regaining lost weight is the first part of the battle. After the initial honeymoon phase you will need to really work to prevent weight gain. In addition to daily exercise and avoiding liquid calories, I suggest drinking six glasses of water and eating no more than three to four times a day.

I have a friend who had gastric bypass surgery about two years ago. She has lost 145 pounds, and now her doctor is recommending a panniculectomy. What is this surgery? Does everyone require it? Will insurance cover it?

Not everyone requires a panniculectomy following gastric bypass surgery, but many people will. After losing a great deal of weight many people are left with as much as ten to twenty pounds of excess skin around their abdomen. This excess skin is called a panniculus.

A panniculus is not just a cosmetic problem; it can cause significant back strain and can lead to very severe skin rashes and infections. It creates major difficulties with personal hygiene as many people are unable to effectively clean between all the folds of skin. There is no doubt that a panniculus is also a cosmetic problem in that it makes it difficult for a person to fit into clothes. This can be very discouraging, especially for a person who has spent a year or more working at weight loss.

Some people require a more extensive procedure called an abdominoplasty. This procedure involves tightening the abdominal wall followed by the removal of excess skin. If your insurance covered your gastric bypass, the provider will probably also recognize the medical necessity of either an abdominoplasty or panniculectomy. Even so, once again your surgeon will need to provide your insurance company with a letter proving medical necessity.

Are there any other surgeries commonly performed following gastric bypass? Are these also routinely covered by insurance?

In addition to panniculectomies and abdominoplasties, many women require reconstructive breast surgery. If this surgery is being recommended due to back, neck, or shoulder pain it may be covered. Likewise if it is being recommended due to infection beneath the breasts it may also be covered. On the other hand, if it is purely cosmetic it is unlikely to be covered.

After the dramatic weight loss achieved with gastric bypass many men and women find themselves with a great deal of redundant skin in the upper arms. Some people call these "batwings." It has been my experience that "batwings" are more troubling to women than men. Unfortunately because "batwings" rarely if ever result in a medical problem, you will be on your own if you choose to have surgery to remove this excess skin. The same is true regarding the removal of excess skin around the buttocks.

Excess skin also occurs in the thigh area. You might have more success in getting coverage for removal of this skin because of the risk of infection or due to its interference with walking. However you should be warned that the incision required to remove excess skin in the thigh area is likely to be quite long. If you have a history of diabetes and poor wound healing, you will want to think twice before having this type of surgery.

All of the aforementioned surgeries are generally performed by plastic surgeons. If you need more information or are looking for a plastic surgeon in your area I suggest you go to the website plasticsurgery.org.

"By taking a risk and having gastric bypass surgery, I changed everything about my life," said Jenny. "I remember the first time I could see the bones in my neck. I remember the first time I flew and didn't need an extension for my seat belt. I remember buying my first medium size top in a mall in Atlanta with my brother. I remember the first time someone I knew didn't recognize me. I remember the first time I looked in the mirror and didn't recognize myself. I remember the smile on my four-year-old nephew's face when he finally realized who I was. I remember tears rolling down my mother's cheeks when she saw me for the first time after my weight loss. And I remember the day Kevin told me how beautiful I was."

During her college years, Jenny suffered a traumatic experience that she struggled with alone for over a year. During that time she gained a tremendous amount of weight. When she ultimately sought help, her counselor suggested that she might be gaining weight to hide. Even though Jenny successfully dealt with her trauma, she continued to gain weight. By the time she completed her master's degree in speech pathology, she was markedly obese.

During her last year of school, on a flight to Seattle to attend the American Speech and Hearing Association conference, Jenny had to ask the flight attendant for an extension for her seat belt. In spite of the humiliation, she forced herself to remain cheerful and upbeat as she wanted to do well in the job interviews—the main reason she was attending the conference.

Jenny graduated with her master's degree in May of 1997. One week later, she had relocated and was working in Maine.

She was warmly received at her new job, but while she quickly made new friends, she never dated. She did her best to avoid putting herself in a position of being embarrassed about her weight, which meant she rarely went out at night. Life was lonely.

When she moved to Maine, Jenny's physician became concerned about her patient's well-being. Jenny was referred to a registered dietitian. The dietitian taught Jenny a regimen that combined diet and water aerobics, and for a year and a half, Jenny followed the program faithfully.

Her inability to lose more than 5 pounds, however, frustrated both of them. Finally, in November of 2000, Jenny's dietitian brought up the idea of gastric bypass. Jenny already knew about the procedure as both her father and her maternal aunt had gone through it. Even though her aunt had multiple complications Jenny was willing to entertain the idea of surgery for herself, even though she didn't think she was large enough to qualify.

At five feet, four and a half inches and 277 pounds, Jenny had a BMI of 48 and from a weight perspective qualified for gastric bypass.

At her first informational meeting she watched a video. "Once I saw that video, I knew I had to have this done. I knew I deserved a chance at a leaner life." She was surprised that she was asked to undergo drug screening at that first visit. She was also required to fill out a questionnaire aimed at evaluating her psychiatric health, an exercise she remembers as "tedious and senseless." The psychologist who evaluated the questionnaire found Jenny to be psychologically sound, but based on the trauma she experienced in college, thought she might benefit from a few sessions with a counselor. This proved to be a worthwhile suggestion. Jenny met a few times with a psychologist who also believed her to be an excellent candidate for surgery. All the while, Jenny continued to work with her nutritionist on her weight loss.

By March Jenny was ready to apply to her insurance company. With the support of her doctors, she was approved within two days. Once approved, Jenny was given a June 4 surgery date. She was also told for the first time about a weight loss requirement. In order to have surgery she was required to lose 10 percent of her body weight.

At first, Jenny thought it was a joke. "That's why I am here," she said. "I worked for over a year and only managed to lose 5 pounds." This new roadblock brought her close to tears: 10 percent of her body weight meant 27 pounds, and she was determined to have her surgery on the appointed date.

Over the next two months Jenny continued to attend support group meetings and to work with her nutritionist. Her weight hardly budged.

Due to a conflict in her surgeon's schedule, Jenny's bypass surgery date needed to be moved up a month. The change in her date meant less time to worry and a relaxation of the weight loss requirement.

On Thursday, May 3, Jenny entered the hospital for her Friday morning surgery. The operation took a full six hours and was done laparoscopically. When she woke up, Jenny had an oxygen mask over her face. The smell of the plastic mask made her feel like vomiting. While the nurses in the recovery room assured her that there was nothing in her stomach to vomit, they still helped her on to her side "just in case." Once they switched her oxygen mask to nasal prongs that delivered oxygen, Jenny felt 100 percent better. What surprised her most was that she really didn't have much pain.

If she was surprised, her mother was shocked. Jenny's father had had terrible postoperative pain, and in fact it took him eight days to walk on his own. In an effort to prevent Jenny from experiencing any pain at all, the nurses suggested a dose of morphine each time she got out of bed and each time they helped her change position.

Aside from being extremely groggy due to the morphine, Jenny was "dying of the heat." There was no doubt the day of her surgery was a very warm May day by Maine standards, but Jenny was from

Louisiana and was used to heat. No one could understand why she was so hot. Finally one of the nurses noticed that the special compression stockings worn to prevent a blood clot were set on heat.

Once she got off the morphine and cooled her hot legs, the rest was smooth sailing. Within twenty-four hours of her surgery Jenny took a shower, put on her own pajamas, walked the halls, and bargained with the nurse to remove the compression stockings (even though they were no longer hot they were still fairly uncomfortable). In exchange for taking off the stockings, Jenny had to get up every two hours and walk—round the clock. She and her mother played cards, read, and talked. Jenny recalls this as a wonderful time with her mother.

The day after the operation, Jenny had to swallow gastrographin, a liquid that shows up on x-rays, to determine that her surgical site was free of leaks. Her reward for swallowing what Jenny says is like "dishwashing liquid" was a little cup of diluted sugar-free juice and a sugar-free Popsicle. The day after surgery she progressed to sugar-free Carnation instant breakfast.

By the time of her discharge two days later, only two small tubes providing drainage from the surgical site remained. When she returned for their removal, she had already lost 16 pounds. Her mother stayed for about a week, and by the time she left, Jenny felt confident doing most things on her own.

At her one-month checkup, Jenny had lost 32 pounds; by the fall she was down by 64, and by Thanksgiving when she saw her family for the first time she had lost 97 pounds. When her mother met her at the airport she burst into tears and immediately called Jenny's dad to tell him how "great" Jenny looked. Now that she has lost a total of 135 pounds Jenny looks at the photos from Thanksgiving and thinks, "Boy, I still had a way to go."

After her surgery, Jenny jumped back into life quickly. She returned to work within two weeks and got back to exercising almost immediately. "One of the reasons I have been so successful with this surgery is I exercise every day." As the weight began to disappear, Jenny became more confident and no longer had to restrict her exercise to water aerobics. These days, there is almost nothing she can't do.

The biggest change was the way people responded to her. No longer was her size the first thing they noticed. No longer did she have to prove constantly that she was hardworking and intelligent. Her own family members also responded differently. Jenny had always known her family loved her, but even with them her weight had been a barrier.

When asked if she has any regrets Jenny, like most gastric bypass patients, answers with an emphatic NO! Are there little difficulties? Yes. First of all, Jenny has become more and more lactose intolerant. Lactose intolerance is quite common following gastric bypass surgery (see Chapter Three), but is generally transient. It should be noted that lactose intolerance is very common in adult Americans, and it is quite possible that Jenny would have eventually had difficulties with milk products anyway. Nonetheless, her lactose intolerance began immediately following her surgery. It started with milk, then ice cream, sour cream, and yogurt. At this point she can tolerate only certain cheeses.

To make matters worse, after being treated with liquid antibiotics for an ear infection this past winter (she has had difficulty with pills since her surgery), Jenny struggled for months with severe abdominal pain. Nothing she took (Beano, Gas-X) helped with the pain.

She finally contacted the Obesity Treatment Center at Catholic Medical Center in Manchester, New Hampshire. After a complete medical evaluation including x-rays, endoscopy, an abdominal ultrasound, blood work, and stool samples it was determined that Jenny's pain was not being caused by an infection or a structural problem.

Jenny wound up having a carbohydrate intolerance. She was put on a carbohydrate-free diet, and for the first time in many months Jenny was pain free. She has gradually begun to incorporate small amounts of carbohydrate back into her diet and is learning her limits. Jenny knew it was important for her to have a caring medical team in her community, and also feels strongly that establishing a relationship with a support group has been crucial to her continued success.

Jenny is happy to enumerate some of the secrets of living with gastric bypass. "Once you are a gastric bypass patient, going to the bathroom is never the same. I can't eat most milk products. I can't eat popcorn. Red meat is out, and soda is impossible. You can never drink with a meal. But the benefits outweigh any difficulties. I never would have met Kevin, I probably never would have had the experience of men whistling at me. I know many women wouldn't like to be whistled at, but if you were never whistled at your whole life and it suddenly happens—then it is a pretty good feeling. I have been given an incredible gift, a second chance, and I am making it work. I love my new life—I am getting married to a wonderful man, and my wedding gown is a size 8!"

CHAPTER SIX

Nutrition

What is the best diet for me to follow prior to surgery?

To lose the weight most bariatric surgery centers require, you will obviously need to restrict calories. Since you will need to restrict sugar (sugar is a simple carbohydrate) following surgery to avoid the dumping syndrome (see Chapter Two), it makes sense to get used to reducing sugar preoperatively. Most centers recommend a reduced fat, high protein diet, which can include a moderate amount of more complex carbohydrates (complex carbohydrates include whole grain breads and cereals and a wide variety of fruits and vegetables). I strongly urge you to get into the habit of drinking mostly water and other low- or no-calorie beverages. You do not want to drink calories. In general people treat calories that they drink differently than calories that they eat. For example, even though a sixty-four-ounce bottle of soda contains a whopping 800 calories we don't treat it as almost half of our 2,000-calorie allowance for the day. In general I would recommend aiming for somewhere between 1,800 and 2,000 calories per day during your preoperative weight loss program. A few days of sample meal plans might look like this:

Day 1

Breakfast

2 slices whole grain toast (whole wheat or multigrain)

1 tablespoon peanut butter

1 orange or ½ grapefruit

8 ounces 1 percent milk

coffee or tea with sugar replacement and fat-free half-and-half or milk

Midmorning Snack

1 banana or 1 cup 120-calorie fat-free, sugar-free yogurt

Lunch

2 slices whole wheat bread

1 ounce low-fat cheese

2 slices turkey, chicken, or lean ham

½ cup baby carrots

2 tablespoons nonfat ranch dressing (for dipping carrots)

1 apple

1 glass water or other noncaloric beverage

Midafternoon Snack

1½ cups (half a bag) light microwave popcorn

Dinner

6 ounces salmon steak

1 small potato

1 teaspoon diet margarine

½ cup asparagus

tossed green salad

1 tablespoon low-fat dressing

½ cup nonfat frozen yogurt

½ cup fresh berries

Evening Snack

2 graham crackers

In planning this menu I tried to choose foods of high nutritional value and density. For example a piece of whole grain bread (such as whole wheat or multigrain) will have more fiber than simple white bread. Studies have shown that high-fiber foods tend to fill people up and keep them that way for a longer time than low-fiber foods. Peanut butter may be a high-fat food, but it contains mostly good fats (those not likely to raise your cholesterol levels). Like fiber, fat helps keep you feeling full for a longer period of time than simple carbohydrates. Peanut butter is also a good source of protein. You will need protein for healing post-operatively. Other sources of protein in the meals above include turkey, chicken, and ham. These are excellent. Salmon isn't necessarily low fat, but the fat in salmon comes from omega-3 fatty acids. This type of fat is known to promote heart health. The fruits and vegetables recommended are loaded with good vitamins and nutrients.

Day 2

Breakfast

1 cup low-sugar cereal (cold or hot)

2 tablespoons raisins

6 slivered almonds

8 ounces low-fat milk

4 ounces orange juice

coffee or tea with sugar substitute and fat-free half-and-half or milk

Midmorning Snack

1 banana

Lunch

1 large field green salad with broccoli, red peppers, carrots, mushrooms, and tomatoes

3 ounces grilled chicken or dry white tuna

1 tablespoon diet salad dressing

1 small whole grain roll or whole wheat English muffin

18 grapes or 1 small orange

Midafternoon Snack

1 low-fat cereal bar

Dinner

1½ cups cooked pasta

⅔ cup tomato basil red sauce

4 ounces ground turkey

2 tablespoons chopped onion

1 clove garlic, minced

1 teaspoon olive oil (Sauté onion and garlic in oil; add
turkey, brown, and add entire mixture to red sauce.)

1 cup mixture of broccoli and cauliflower

water or noncaloric beverage

1 cup flavored Italian ice or ½ cup lemon sorbet

Evening Snack

10 animal crackers

8 ounces low-fat milk

1 apple or 4 ounces applesauce

Day 3

Breakfast

1 egg (cooked any way using cooking spray)

1 whole wheat English muffin

2 teaspoons diet tub margarine

1 orange

coffee or tea with sugar substitute and fat-free half-
and-half or milk

Midmorning Snack

½ cup low-fat cottage cheese

½ cup pineapple chunks

Lunch

Lean Cuisine, Weight Watchers, or Healthy Choice
 TV dinner (These do tend to be somewhat high in
 sodium but are perfectly acceptable unless you are
 following a strict sodium restricted diet.)

1 slice whole grain toast

1 teaspoon diet margarine

1 apple or 15 cherries

1 cup 120-calorie fat-free, sugar-free yogurt

water or noncaloric drink

Midafternoon Snack

6 low-fat crackers

1 ounce low-fat cheese

Dinner

6 ounces shrimp (Many people have heard that shrimp
 is too high in cholesterol. It is high in cholesterol but
 low in fat—making it an excellent choice.)

2 cloves fresh garlic, minced

2 teaspoons olive oil (Use to sauté garlic and shrimp.)

¾ cup cooked fettuccini (Place shrimp/garlic mixture
 on fettuccini.)

field greens with tomatoes, red and orange peppers,
 and cucumber

1 teaspoon olive oil mixed with 1 tablespoon balsamic
 vinegar (Toss on greens.)

1 cup steamed broccoli

water or noncaloric beverage

Evening Snack

1 bowl low-sugar cold cereal

8 ounces low-fat milk

To be sure, your diet following surgery will be much more restrictive than this. Nonetheless, for most people the above diet plan will achieve weight loss prior to surgery. For the most part I have included a beverage at every meal. This too will change following surgery. After surgery, your stomach pouch will be so small that you won't be able to manage both food and drink at a single meal. Liquids (mainly water) will need to be consumed between meals. Presurgery, drinking water with your meal will help fill you up and might prevent second helpings. Likewise many people find sipping a clear liquid broth or eating a low-calorie soup fifteen minutes prior to a meal helps curb their appetite. If you find that you are still very hungry after consuming the amount of food allowed in the meal plans above, supplement with a clear broth or other low-calorie soup. Another good choice is salad greens with a fat-free dressing before a meal. During your presurgery weight loss program, get into the habit of eating very slowly. Consider using a baby fork and spoon and a luncheon size plate for dinner.

What will I be able to eat after surgery?

Your diet following surgery will be radically different from the diet I just outlined. Your new stomach will hold between one and two ounces. Over time your stomach will stretch a bit allowing you to eat a little more at any given time. So it is important to take advantage of your very small stomach right after surgery and aim to lose as much weight as possible during your first few postoperative months.

Immediately following surgery you will be given small sips of water and ice chips. Depending on the bariatric center you choose, you may remain on just water for up to a week. Part of this depends on whether or not your surgeon is concerned with the possibility of a leak at the connection between your new stomach pouch and your intestines. If a leak is suspected, you may be brought back to the operating room, or if the leak is very small your doctor might prefer to let it close on its own. In the latter case you will only be allowed sips of water.

Stage 1 (Clear Liquids Only)

Much of the following dietary information (especially the valuable tips) has been provided by Jacquie Cuddihy, R.D., of the Obesity Treatment Center at Catholic Medical Center, Manchester, New Hampshire.

Once your doctor decides you can progress beyond the water/ice chips only diet, you will move on to clear liquids. As you progress with clear liquids you will gradually work up to sipping a quarter cup of one of these liquids at a time. The goal is to get in two ounces or so every thirty minutes while awake. This will help you avoid dehydration. Fluids such as diluted cranberry juice, apple juice, herbal teas, and chicken broth and "foods" like sugar-free Popsicles and diet Jell-O are considered clear liquids because you can see through them. A clear liquid diet may also include sugar-free sorbet, decaffeinated coffee and tea, and of course water. Generally speaking, you will remain on clear liquids as your only source of calories for about two or three days, but this stage can last as long as two to three weeks. Occasionally the sugar in apple and cranberry juice can precipitate the dumping syndrome or vomiting. In this case, dilute the juice with water or switch to only sugar-free products. Many people lose a considerable amount of weight during this clear liquid phase.

Jacquie's Tips for Success at This Stage

- Since carbonated liquids can put pressure on your pouch, all liquids need to be noncarbonated.
- Do *not* chew gum.
- Juice should be diluted to half strength with water to avoid the dumping syndrome (see Chapter Two).
- Do *not* force yourself to keep sipping if you are full.
- Avoid straws. Sipping through them will increase pressure within your pouch.
- Avoid very hot or very cold beverages as they may cause stomach discomfort.
- Resist the urge to ask a friend or family member to bring you a snack. At this stage your new stomach pouch cannot handle food and you must develop a new way of eating.

Stage 2 (Full Liquids)

The next stage in your postoperative dietary progression will be full liquids. Full liquids include things like plain yogurt, sugar-free light yogurts (lemon, vanilla—at this stage you should avoid yogurt with fruit or seeds), cream of wheat or rice cereal, very thin oatmeal, cream of tomato soup, strained cream of chicken soup, and sugar-free pudding. You can also drink anything from the clear liquids group as well. Pitfalls at this stage include the development of lactose intolerance. This often occurs following gastric bypass surgery and means that cream-based soups and cereal with milk will cause significant abdominal cramping, flatulence, and diarrhea. If this occurs, these foods should be avoided. Luckily, for most people lactose intolerance is a temporary problem, which generally resolves within weeks to a few months. Also while tomato soup may be okay, some people find tomato products and orange or grapefruit juice a little too acidic. During the full liquid stage you will consume a total of a half cup of "food" per meal. If you become full before you have finished the entire half cup, do not force yourself to finish. Doing so could result in vomiting. During the full liquid stage and in all subsequent stages you will want to avoid drinking water (or any clear liquid) with your meal. If you do so you will become too full too quickly. In order to ensure proper nutrition and healing related to surgery you will now begin drinking a daily protein drink. You should ask the nutritionist at your center which protein drink is right for you. The full liquid stage generally lasts one to three weeks. Once again, many people lose a considerable amount of weight during this phase.

Jacquie's Tips

- If you experience lactose intolerance (described earlier) contact the dietitian at your center. He or she will help you develop a milk-free diet for the next few months.

- Stop eating as soon as you begin to feel full. If you try to keep eating you are likely to feel very uncomfortable and may vomit.

- You should continue to avoid carbonated beverages, gum, straws, and very hot or very cold beverages.

Jacquie's Sample Full Liquid Menu

Breakfast

3 tablespoons cream of wheat

3 tablespoons plain yogurt

Lunch

2 tablespoons low-fat strained cream soup

2 tablespoons sugar-free pudding

2 tablespoons light yogurt

Dinner

3 tablespoons low-fat strained cream soup

3 tablespoons sugar-free pudding

In between meals it is very important to sip water or other sugar-free beverages to avoid dehydration. At this stage your goal is to consume six to eight cups of fluid per day.

Stage 3 (Pureed and Soft Foods)

Pureed and soft foods include low-fat or nonfat cottage cheese, low-fat or nonfat sugar-free yogurt, pureed chicken, tuna, or turkey, scrambled eggs, low-fat ricotta cheese, unsweetened applesauce, pureed fruits such as pears and peaches, pureed vegetables such as broccoli, carrots, and beans, hummus, mashed potatoes, oatmeal, cream of wheat, tofu, strained baby fruit (unsweetened), and fruit smoothies.

It is important to get your protein in before high-carbohydrate foods. This should become a permanent habit. If you simply ate the high-carbohydrate foods listed above (fruits, cereals, vegetables), you would not get in the protein you need to heal from your surgery and stay healthy for the long haul.

In addition at this stage the high-carbohydrate foods may cause the dumping syndrome (see Chapter Two), which is very unpleasant. At each meal during the pureed and soft food stage, you will take in about three-quarters cup of food. You will need to eat very slowly. If you get full before you have finished eating the entire amount, do not push yourself to eat more as doing so might result in vomiting.

The pureed food stage will also last two to three weeks. Again remember to drink water in between your meals. I recommend that you try to get at least sixty-four ounces of water in between meals per day.

Jacquie's Tips

- Do not drink fluids with meals.
- Wait thirty minutes after a meal before drinking.
- Eat very slowly.
- Chew food well.
- Eat protein foods first.
- Continue to observe tips from Stages 1 and 2.

Jacquie's Sample Pureed Foods Menu

Breakfast

½ cup scrambled eggs

¼ cup low-fat or nonfat yogurt

Lunch

½ cup low-fat or nonfat cottage cheese

¼ cup unsweetened applesauce

Dinner

½ cup pureed chicken

¼ cup mashed potatoes

In Stage 3 you will begin to take your vitamin and mineral supplements. Begin with two chewable complete children's vitamins per day or one chewable complete adult vitamin per day. The vitamin should be chewed very well before swallowing. After about two months you will be able to swallow pills. You will also begin taking a calcium supplement. I recommend taking at least 1,500 mg of calcium citrate with vitamin D per day. The preferred form of calcium is calcium citrate as it is the form of calcium that is best absorbed. Your calcium supplement will also need to be chewed, crushed, or dissolved in water. Finally, at this stage you will also begin taking vitamin B_{12}. Some health food and drug stores carry sublingual vitamin B_{12} (dissolves under your tongue).

Stage 4 (Chopped Moist Foods)

Depending on how rapidly you have progressed through the first three stages you may be as little as four to five weeks or as long as ten weeks out from your life-changing surgery. At this point you probably feel ready for real food. You are almost there. The average size of a meal will now be a full cup. As in all other stages, and in fact for the rest of your life, you should eat your protein first. This stage introduces many new foods. In addition to the foods and fluids from the previous three stages you may now add the following foods:

low-fat cheese

white fish (flaked)

egg, whole (chopped)

moist poultry (chopped or ground)

tuna (packed in water)

tuna, chicken, ham, or egg salad (made with nonfat mayonnaise)

legumes — beans and lentils (mashed)

winter squash

baked potato without skin

carrots (well cooked and mashed)

spinach (well cooked and chopped)

unsweetened canned peaches (chopped)

unsweetened canned pears (chopped)

toast

plain crackers

unsweetened dry cereals (soaked in skim or 1 percent milk)

Jacquie's Tips

- Eat three meals per day and do *not* snack between meals.

- Chew foods to a mushy consistency.

- Remember to eat slowly.
- Continue to take all vitamin and mineral supplements.
- Drink at least forty-eight to sixty-four ounces of fluid (water is best) over the course of the day.
- Stop eating when you feel full.
- Take bites the size of a pencil eraser.

Jacquie's Sample Menu

Breakfast

1 egg (prepared any way)

¼ cup cereal

¾ cup skim or 1 percent milk

Lunch

½ cup tuna

¼ cup yogurt

¼ cup peaches (If canned, the peaches should be packed in their own juice.)

Dinner

2 ounces ground moist chicken with fat-free gravy

¼ cup mashed potatoes

¼ cup mashed carrots

Stage 5 (Real Food—at Last!)

You may have spent between twelve and twenty-two weeks getting to this stage. You are looking forward to getting back to real food. As you enter this stage, it is important to remember that although you will now begin to eat "real food," things will never be as they were before your operation.

During this stage you will probably discover that certain foods—even foods you may have loved in the past—will no longer appeal. Certain foods—some predictable, like sweets, some unique to you—may make you ill. Megan, whom you read about in Chapter Three, told me that the best advice she received prior to her gastric bypass was to always try new foods at home. It wasn't until Megan vomited in a restaurant that she understood the importance of this advice. After that embarrassing experience Megan will not risk trying a new food anywhere but at home.

The major difference between the Stage 5 diet and the Stage 4 diet is the fact that now all the foods are whole foods. Because of this you will need to chew thoroughly before swallowing. I am sure I sound like a broken record, but as with all other stages remember to eat your protein first.

Rather than give you specific menus, the following is a summary of foods you will now be eating. I do give you some ideas for food choices at meals, but I will leave the specific choices to you. I think you are ready.

Protein: eggs, fish, chicken, ham, low-fat cheeses, low-fat cottage cheese, tofu, and yogurt.

Starches: white potato, sweet potato, squash, pasta, unsweetened cereals, crackers, toast, pita bread, beans, and lentils.

Vegetables: soft-cooked *plain* vegetables.

Fruits: unsweetened canned fruits, fresh fruit as tolerated. Canned fruits really should be unsweetened (the can may say "packed in their own juice"). Fruit packed in syrup is likely to cause the dumping syndrome.

Fats: small amounts of low-fat margarine, oil, low-fat salad dressing, nonfat/low-fat mayonnaise, nonfat/low-fat sour cream, and low-fat cream cheese.

Beverages: coffee, tea, nonfat/low-fat milk, diet soda can be introduced.

Miscellaneous: salt, pepper, herbs, and other seasoning as desired and tolerated.

Because your diet is now more varied you will no longer require the daily protein drink. A typical breakfast might include one scrambled egg followed by a small amount (a quarter cup) of fruit or half a slice of toast. Lunch might consist of one of the following: two ounces tuna, turkey, or chicken, four ounces low-fat, sugar-free yogurt, four ounces low-fat cottage cheese, or a slice of low-fat cheese followed by a quarter of a pita pocket and a quarter cup of cooked carrots and half a skinless peach. Homemade low-fat soups with lean meats or beans are a good option for lunch or dinner. Dinner might be two to three ounces of lean meat or fish followed by a quarter cup of mashed potatoes, a quarter cup of a vegetable, and a quarter of a banana.

Listen to your body and stop eating when you are full. Learn to eat slowly. In our hurried life, this is something that is difficult to master. Eating slowly serves two purposes: first, you actually learn to enjoy the texture and flavor or the food you are eating, and second, you are less likely to overeat and vomit. Some people find it helpful to eat using baby utensils and dishes, or try placing your utensil down while chewing. Your bites should be the size of a pencil eraser and should be chewed thoroughly. Once again, in order to prevent dehydration, remember to drink plenty of water between meals.

I have already mentioned this, but it is worth repeating here in the diet section. You will need lifelong supplementation with the following vitamins and minerals: calcium with or without vitamin D, vitamin B_{12}, iron, and a multivitamin with minerals.

Jacquie's Observations

Food intolerances seem to be very individual. However, foods that frequently give people trouble include red meats, pasta, bread, rice, tough or dry chicken and turkey, as well as raw fruits and vegetables.

Jacquie's Tips for Continued Success

- Avoid potato skins even though they are rich in nutrients; they tend to be very difficult to tolerate.

- Avoid high-fat or fried foods. Not only are these high in calories, they tend to cause significant stomach upset.

- Avoid alcohol. Many people find that even small amounts of alcohol can be quite intoxicating.

- Eat very slowly. As a general rule of thumb, it should take you about ten minutes to eat an ounce of food. If you are eating eight ounces of food at a meal, plan on at least an hour. An hour and twenty minutes would be the ideal.

- Avoid high-calorie drinks such as fruit juice, frappes, and soda. If these are consumed frequently you will see your weight climb.

- Avoid stretching your new stomach pouch. The amount of food the pouch can hold will gradually increase over a period of six to nine months. However if you continuously eat to the point of vomiting it will stretch more significantly and could defeat the purpose of the surgery.

- Avoid snacks. Eat three meals a day and drink calorie-free beverages in between. While a bedtime snack is probably fine and can be worked into your diet, eating small snacks continuously throughout the day is a surefire way to gain weight—don't do it. One woman who lost one hundred pounds over a period of eight months gradually gained back all but twenty pounds. How did she do it? She found that continuous snacking on tiny pieces of chocolate candy didn't cause dumping. She developed a habit of eating a pound bag of chocolate candy per day, and before she knew it she was practically back where she started.

- If you haven't done so already, develop a daily aerobic exercise program. Anyone can lose weight with a diet—the people most successful at keeping weight off are those people who exercise daily.

I know people who were eating "real" food within a week of having gastric bypass surgery—why is it necessary to progress so slowly through these stages?

There is no doubt that most people get bored with introducing foods very slowly, and as with all "diets" most people cheat. One of my patients ate pizza within a week of surgery, and another ate a chicken wing. These foods were certainly not on their menu. In the long run, although there is certainly some flexibility in the rate of dietary progression following surgery, I think people who stick as closely as possible to the diet outlined by their personal dietitian will be the most successful at achieving their desired weight—and keeping it off—and will have the fewest complications.

What should a typical daily menu look like twelve months after surgery?

Your goal should be to consume no more than 1,000 to 1,200 calories per day. The following might represent a typical few days:

Day 1

Breakfast

1 cup low-fat, sugar-free yogurt (120 calories per 8-ounce cup)

½ banana, sliced

Beverage Between Breakfast and Noon

1 eight-ounce glass water and/or 1 cup coffee or tea (optional: with fat-free half-and-half)

Lunch

3 ounces sliced chicken or turkey

½ whole wheat pita pocket

¼ cup cooked vegetable

1 teaspoon reduced fat mayonnaise

Beverage Between Lunch and Dinner

1 eight-ounce glass water and/or 1 eight-ounce glass
sugar-free, decaffeinated ice tea

Dinner

4 ounces shrimp cocktail with cocktail sauce

½ cup rice pilaf

½ cup asparagus

1 tablespoon light tub margarine

Evening Snack

1 ounce reduced fat cheddar cheese

½ peeled apple

Beverage Before Bed

1 or 2 eight-ounce glasses water or other diet
beverage

Day 2

Breakfast

¼ cup Egg Beaters or 2 egg white omelet with ½ ounce
grated low-fat cheddar cheese and ½ cup of a mixture of peeled and chopped red and yellow peppers
(mix ingredients and cook in a pan sprayed with
cooking spray—add salt and pepper to taste)

½ slice whole wheat toast topped with spray margarine

Beverage Between Breakfast and Lunch

2 glasses water or 1 glass water and 1 cup caffeinated
   or decaffeinated tea or coffee

Lunch

Low-calorie microwavable dinner such as Lean
   Cuisine, Weight Watchers, or Healthy Choice

Beverage Between Lunch and Dinner

1 or 2 glasses of water or other low-calorie beverage

Dinner

3 ounces grilled tuna

½ cup couscous

1 teaspoon diet tub margarine

½ cup broccoli or summer squash

Evening Snack

1 graham cracker topped with 1 to 2 teaspoons natural
   peanut butter

4 ounces skim milk

Beverage Before Bed

1 eight-ounce glass water

This diet may sound strict now, especially if you are reading this book in preparation for surgery, but you won't be
as hungry as you were before surgery. Even though you
won't be as hungry, however, many people still miss the ability to overeat. One of my patients told me that he wished he

could reverse the surgery on Thanksgiving and other "big eating" holidays. Obviously this is not possible. It may take time and you may actually long for the "good old days" sometimes, but at the end of the day on Thanksgiving when you don't feel like a stuffed pig or you haven't vomited because you ate too much, you will be glad that you had your surgery and practiced some restraint.

When Laura entered the hospital on Tuesday, March 25, she was obviously nervous. Her last operation had been a tonsillectomy at the age of five, so this one was a little different. "Frankly, the thing that scared me the most was getting an intravenous line." Laura had seen her father getting "stuck" for an IV many times and it always looked so awful. But even the IV wasn't as bad as she'd feared—and almost before she knew it, she was waking up in the recovery room.

The initial half hour was uncomfortable as she experienced some pain at the incision, but with medication things quickly improved. The first day she was given moist swabs (not even ice chips), and within twenty-four hours she went down for her gastrographin swallow to check for any leaks at the surgical site. Since everything looked fine, her diet progressed to sips of water on Wednesday. Thursday one of the nurses brought her diluted apple juice, which felt fine going down but ended up causing significant nausea (probably due to the sugar in the juice). She began walking the day of surgery and by Friday, having proven to the surgical staff that she could climb stairs (which she had at home), she was discharged.

Laura's mother stayed with her for the first day but left at night. One thing that Laura noticed that first day home was just how tired and spacey she felt. She soon realized that the way she felt didn't have anything to do with her surgery but was due to the fact that she had abruptly stopped a medication she had been taking prior to surgery.

After her doctor said she could get back on it, she immediately felt better.

The only other medication-related problem Laura experienced was with Percocet, the pain medication she was given on discharge. Soon after taking it, Laura was visited by "panthers," in one of the most vivid nightmares of her life. Once the pills were flushed down the toilet, Laura was on the road to recovery. In fact, since surgery her blood pressure has been perfect and she no longer requires any medication.

Not one to sit still, Laura and her mother went out shopping within a week. On the way back they decided to go to one of their favorite Chinese restaurants. Laura ordered wonton soup and ate only the broth and then, in a daring move, she ate a chicken wing (without the skin). Surprisingly it stayed down. For the most part, however, she followed the meal plan outlined by the dietitian at the Obesity Treatment Center. "I stuck to the meal plan but moved from stage to stage a little quicker than many people—by the time I was e-mailed the Stage 4 diet, I was already on it."

Laura is now almost five months out from surgery. Including the twenty-six pounds she lost before the procedure, she is ninety pounds lighter and plans to lose another forty or fifty pounds. She has not weighed this little since she graduated from high school over twenty years ago, and this time she knows it's off to stay. "This time it doesn't feel like a diet—it feels permanent, like a new way of life."

And for Laura her weight loss has brought a new sense of adventure and confidence. "In the past I was tired all the time. I'd come home from work, turn on the television, eat dinner, go to bed, and start all over again in the morning. Now I am more open to going out, I always want to be doing something. It could be as simple as taking the dog on a long walk, going to exercise class, or a social event. I am looking forward to a trip to Hawaii with my mother and a group of friends. I can't wait to get in the plane and not have to ask for a seat belt extension!"

Exercise

Once I have surgery, what kind of an exercise program should I be striving for?

After surgery the best exercise program is the one you will stick with. For many people, daily exercise means the difference between achieving their ideal weight and settling for a less dramatic success. In addition, as I noted earlier, without exercise, many people begin to gain some weight back after about a year of consistent weight loss.

Exercise can improve your overall health. It can also markedly improve blood pressure, diabetes, and triglyceride levels. If you haven't initiated an exercise program preoperatively, you should begin in earnest the day after surgery. Walking from day one is designed to prevent complications such as blood clots related to the surgery, but you can think of it as the first day of the new you. And if you have already been walking a bit preoperatively, walking the day after surgery will not be such a daunting task.

As you plan out your postsurgery exercise program it is important to keep three things in mind: frequency, intensity, and time (also known as the F.I.T. principle).

Frequency

How frequently you exercise will differ depending on your fitness goals. Since your goal is weight loss, you will ultimately need to exercise a minimum of six times a week.

Intensity

To make the most of your exercise program it is important to work at the proper intensity. Intensity is how hard you are pushing yourself. You want to be working hard enough to achieve a training effect, that is, replacing fat with muscle, but not so hard that your body kicks into anaerobic metabolism.

How can you tell if you are exercising at the proper intensity? Measuring your heart rate to determine whether you are within your target range is simple. It's all about your pulse. One way is by checking your pulse and determining your target heart rate. You can check your pulse in any number of locations—your neck, wrist, behind your knee, or on your foot. These pulses are called the carotid, radial, popliteal, and dorsalis pedis respectively. Your pulse is simply your heart rate. Each beat of your heart creates a pulse, which you can feel and count.

As an example, right now find your pulse by placing your index and middle fingers on the thumb side of your wrist. Here you will feel your radial pulse. Count the number of pulses over a ten-second period and multiply that by six. This gives you your pulse or heart rate per minute. Your heart rate (the number of times your heart beats per minute) is an indirect measurement of how hard you are exercising. The target heart rate (THR) range is a common method of measuring exercise intensity. In order to determine your target heart rate, you will first need to calculate your maximum heart rate.

To figure your maximum heart rate use the following formula:

220 − your age = maximum heart rate (MHR)

For example, for a 50-year-old male or female

220 − 50 = 170 beats per minute

In order to lose weight and achieve physical fitness it is not necessary to work out at your maximum heart rate; in fact this would be undesirable, especially as you begin a regular exercise program. Studies have determined that exercising at a heart rate of between 50 and 85 percent of your maximum heart rate is sufficient to produce excellent results and a training effect. Again using the same 50-year-old man or woman to determine the THR use the following equations:

170 × 0.50 = 85 beats per minute

170 × 0.85 = 145 beats per minute

The THR range is therefore 85 to 145 beats per minute.

Table 7.1 will help you determine your own target heart rate and ten-second pulse.

Some people have a great deal of difficulty measuring their pulse. Still others are on blood pressure medications,

TABLE 7.1 Target Heart Rates

Age	Maximum HR	Target HR	10-second pulse
20	200	100–170	17–28
25	195	98–166	17–28
30	190	95–162	16–27
35	185	92–157	16–27
40	180	90–153	15–26
45	175	88–149	15–26
50	170	85–145	14–25
55	165	82–140	14–25
60	160	80–136	13–24
65	155	78–131	13–24
70	150	75–128	12–23
75	145	72–123	12–23
80	140	70–119	11–22

which slow the heart rate. Beta-blockers for example generally drop the pulse to 60 beats per minute or less. People on beta-blockers may find it impossible to achieve their target heart rate with exercise. This does not mean they should not exercise or if they do that they will not be able to accurately assess the intensity of their program.

The "Talk Test" is by far the easiest (and a fairly accurate) method of determining whether a person is exercising at the appropriate intensity to achieve aerobic fitness. As you are exercising, you should be able to talk without huffing and puffing excessively. On the other hand, if you could easily deliver the Gettysburg Address, you need to push a little harder.

Time

You will need (and want) to spend enough time on your exercise program to achieve cardiovascular fitness and to promote weight loss. The bare minimum is thirty minutes, three times a week (not including warm-up and cooldown times). But for most of my patients, this is not enough. In general we find weight loss and weight maintenance requires a commitment of forty-five to sixty minutes per day, six to seven days a week. This is true if you choose walking as your exercise. If, however, you choose a higher intensity activity like a stair-climber, jogging/running, Nordic track, kick-boxing, or a spin class, you can probably lose weight or maintain your weight loss with just thirty minutes per day. My recommendation is to begin with walking. Choose the more intense exercises once you have lost forty or fifty pounds. This will protect your hips, knees, and ankles from excessive stress and strain.

Some people who are either short on time or who have difficulty exercising for a full forty-five to sixty minutes ask me if it is possible to do more shorter sessions over the course of the day. There is mounting evidence that a few short exercise sessions during a day provide a person with the same weight loss impact as one long session. This knowledge allows a person to progress more quickly through the initial conditioning and improvement stages of developing an exercise program.

Developing Your Exercise Program

Now you that you are ready to begin an exercise program, it's important to plan it out. But remember nothing is in stone. The American College of Sports Medicine (ACSM) defines three stages of an aerobic exercise program. The stages include an initial conditioning stage (approximately the first four to six weeks — however, if you have not exercised in a while, please extend this stage by another four weeks) followed by an improvement stage (anywhere from twelve to twenty-four weeks). The final stage, maintenance, is meant to last a lifetime.

Many people continue to become more fit even during the maintenance phase, and it is during this phase that new types of exercises may be attempted. When you reach the maintenance phase it is very likely that you will still be losing weight at a rapid pace and may still be recovering from your surgery. Although many people consider training for a road race or bike race once they reach the maintenance phase, I suggest waiting until your weight has reached a relatively stable point before getting involved in a competitive event. As you progress through the stages remember the recommended rate of progression is not set in stone. Some people will get bored with the initial conditioning phase and will want to move on to the improvement phase within two weeks, whereas another person might spend twelve to sixteen weeks working on the initial conditioning phase. Since you will be recovering from a surgical procedure I suggest taking things slowly. You have the rest of your life, the important thing is daily exercise. Take your time, listen to your body, and you will progress at the right pace. As you develop your exercise plan, it is crucial to discuss your initial plan and your plans for progression with your personal physician.

The next few pages will help you plan an exercise program. The focus will be on a walking program, but other forms of aerobic exercise are perfectly acceptable as long as they allow you to achieve your desired heart rate and fitness goals. In fact, many people may initially find walking difficult due to knee or back problems. As you lose weight walking becomes easier. Early on you may want to consider water walking, as this is much easier on your bones and joints. Most large gyms will have a pool with a walking lane.

Again, before you jump into the exercise program outlined below be sure to discuss your exercise plan with your surgeon and personal physician.

Initial Conditioning Phase

During the initial conditioning phase two things are crucial: consistency and patience. You will not improve if you only exercise once a week. Conversely, if you jump into exercise and try to work out seven days a week, sixty minutes per session, you may well experience an overuse injury. I suggest the program outlined in Table 7.2. You should begin this exercise program immediately following surgery.

I suggest trying to push for five times a week if your goal is maximum weight loss. Table 7.3 gives you your target heart rate range for the initial conditioning phase. If you have not exercised in many years I suggest extending this phase by four weeks. If this is your situation you may want to plan to walk for ten minutes, three to five times a week for the first four weeks, aiming for 50 to 60 percent of MHR. After these initial four weeks jump into the program as outlined above.

TABLE 7.2 Exercise Schedule for Initial Conditioning Phase

Weeks	Frequency	Intensity	Time
1–2	3–5 times a week	50–60% MHR	15 minutes
3–4	3–5 times a week	50–60% MHR	15–18 minutes
5–6	3–5 times a week	50–60% MHR	18–20 minutes

MHR = Maximum Heart Rate. Your target heart rate is 50 to 60 percent of the MHR (see Table 7.3).

TABLE 7.3 Target Heart Rates for Initial Conditioning Phase

Age	50–60% MHR	10-second pulse
20	100–120	17–20
25	98–117	17–20
30	95–114	16–19
35	92–111	16–19
40	90–108	15–18
45	88–105	15–18
50	85–102	14–17
55	82–99	14–17
60	80–96	13–16
65	78–93	13–16
70	75–90	12–15
75	72–87	12–15
80	70–84	11–14
85	68–81	11–14

You are now ready to move to the improvement stage (see Table 7.4). On average this stage will last anywhere between twelve and twenty-four weeks. Again, you decide how quickly to progress.

During the improvement stage it is up to you to determine your goals. If you want to achieve the most in terms of weight loss, I suggest working up to a frequency of six to seven sessions per week. Let your body guide you regard-

TABLE 7.4 Exercise Schedule for Improvement Stage

Weeks	Frequency	Intensity	Time
7–10	4–5 times a week	60–70% MHR	20 minutes
11–14	4–5 times a week	70–80% MHR	25 minutes
15–20	5–6 times a week	70–85% MHR	30 minutes
21–25	6–7 times a week	70–85% MHR	45–60 minutes

ing intensity. It is perfectly acceptable to continue at 50 to 60 percent of the MHR during the improvement stage. The target heart rates for the improvement stage are listed in Table 7.5.

The maintenance stage requires persistence and commitment. You have acquired the skills necessary to maintain an exercise program for life. Staying committed is now the challenge. Some people find that working with a partner sustains enthusiasm. Many people find someone in their weight loss support group to walk with. Other people reward themselves with a prize if they accumulate a certain number of miles per month. Charting mileage is fun. One of my patients set a yearlong goal to walk one thousand miles. She figured out where that would be traveling south from her home and plotted her weekly progress on a AAA map. At the end of the year she and her husband flew there for a vacation.

TABLE 7.5 Target Heart Rates for Improvement Stage

Age	60–85% MHR	10-second pulse
20	120–170	20–28
25	117–166	20–28
30	114–162	19–27
35	111–157	19–27
40	108–153	18–26
45	105–149	18–26
50	102–145	17–25
55	99–140	17–25
60	96–136	16–24
65	93–131	16–24
70	90–128	15–23
75	87–123	15–23
80	84–119	14–22
85	81–115	14–22

Another way to stay excited about exercise is to train for a worthy cause. Walking for the American Heart Association Walk or other charitable events can give your workout a whole new energy and sense of purpose.

Finally, depending upon where you live in this country you must plan how you will continue to maintain your exercise program during the winter months. An excellent idea is to purchase a treadmill, but be sure it's an electric one. Self-propelled treadmills are very difficult to work with and as a result people give up. Some people join a gym in the winter. Still others walk at a local mall or high school. Many malls or high schools open early to accommodate walkers.

In general, during the maintenance stage you should plan on walking six to seven times a week at 70 to 85 percent of your MHR. Each session should last about sixty minutes. Again, you can customize this according to your fitness goals.

Because you will want to continue your exercise program for the rest of your life it is crucial to take steps to avoid injury. Performing a warm-up and cooldown are two very important components of your exercise program. For many people who want to jump right into their exercise routine this can seem tedious. I assure you, they are essential.

The warm-up consists of a five- to ten-minute period of either stretching or a less intense version of whatever your chosen exercise is. I generally recommend a slow walk. This slow walk allows your body to reach your target heart rate (whatever it may be) safely and comfortably.

The cooldown helps slow your heart down gradually. Over the course of a five- to ten-minute slow walk you should be able to bring your heart rate fairly close to your pre-exercise heart rate. Slowing your heart rate gradually helps prevent blood from pooling in your legs, greatly reducing the risk of fainting and lightheadedness. Stretching is also a good idea during the cooldown phase of your program.

Remember, the warm-up and cooldown phases of your exercise session do not count toward total time exercised. If you are aiming for a sixty-minute program, the warm-up and cooldown can add between ten and twenty minutes.

I have saved my most important advice for the end of the chapter. As you embark on an exercise program it is important to be patient with yourself. You may not have enjoyed exercise in the past, but if you give yourself eight to twelve weeks (that puts you into the improvement stage) you will find that your body can do more than you ever thought it could. You will become proud of what you have accomplished. You may hate to admit it, but you will begin to enjoy walking (or biking or swimming—whatever exercise you have chosen). Even if you don't quite get to the point of *liking* exercise, consider this: One of my patients told me, "There is nothing like having exercised." After a year of regular exercise, he still didn't enjoy the program, but he knew he needed it and was committed to continuing. His trick was to exercise first thing in the morning so that he could get it over with and then start his day with that satisfying feeling of "having already exercised."

Hopefully you will find exercise more enjoyable than my patient but no matter how you accomplish it, exercise is crucial to weight maintenance. Almost everyone will lose weight following a gastric bypass, but in my experience the only people who actually achieve their ideal body weight are those who exercise at least six or seven days a week. Why not head out today to buy a good pair of walking shoes — you will then be ready to begin getting started on the trip toward better health.

"I come from a family of eaters," Pat explains. "We eat when we are sad, we eat when we are happy—everything calls for food."

When Pat reached 297 pounds, he joined a medically supervised weight loss program and managed to drop down to 244. Unfortunately, as is all too frequently the case, the weight crept right back on. In October of 1999, at 312 pounds, Pat began complaining of fatigue and shoulder pain, which can be symptoms of underlying heart disease.

The stress test (see Chapter Four) we ordered was abnormal and he subsequently underwent a heart catheterization (a procedure in which dye is injected into the coronary arteries via a thin, hollow plastic tube to determine if they are blocked).

The catheterization was not reassuring. There were at least four very significant blockages in his heart arteries. A bypass operation (open-heart surgery in which a vein from the leg or an artery from the breast is used to connect the aorta with a coronary artery just beyond the blockage) was recommended.

Since Pat was in no immediate danger, he decided to go home and think about his options. He already knew he had to go through with the cardiac bypass. But he also knew he had to confront the larger issue: he had to tackle his obesity.

Soon after his cardiac bypass, Pat and I began discussing gastric bypass surgery. He listened carefully as I described the procedure, and he clearly understood the risks and the potential benefits of this surgery. To him, gastric bypass had nothing to do with looking better—it was about becoming healthier and living longer.

I was amused to discover that Pat never thought of himself as overweight: "I just thought of myself as a big, strong, Irish guy," he said. Once he had made the decision to undergo a gastric bypass, he didn't feel the need to read extensively about the procedure. Nor was he particularly nervous. He approached surgery in the same matter-of-fact way he approached life. He understood that his weight was a major health problem, one that he had been unable to tackle on his own. He understood that gastric bypass was a tool that would allow him to lose weight. Most importantly, he understood that once he had the procedure, it would be up to him to keep the weight off long-term.

In December of 2000, Pat called the gastric bypass program at New England Medical Center (NEMC) and requested an appointment. He was surprised that the first available opening was not until August. Due to the overwhelming interest in gastric bypass, this is the norm for many programs. Since his work schedule had some flexibility, he asked to be contacted if there was a cancellation, and four months later he got lucky.

Pat met with the team at NEMC in March and was scheduled for an August surgery date. Once again, however, a cancellation allowed an earlier date. In June 2001, he went to NEMC for a day of laboratory testing and gallbladder evaluation. He had been given cardiac clearance from my group so further cardiac evaluation was unnecessary. He had no history of snoring, so a sleep study was also deemed unnecessary.

His surgery was finally scheduled for the fifth of July. Pat doesn't recall being nervous or frightened. He believed he was doing the right thing and knew he was in good hands. He felt confident that he would make it through surgery. And although he knew that no surgery is without risk, the prospect of a longer, healthier life made the risk worth taking.

Pat sailed through surgery. The procedure itself took about four hours and was done via a laparoscope. He left the hospital on July 7, 2001—his fifty-first birthday, a coincidence he saw as a sign that he had conquered the McCarthy legacy of an early death: he was going to outlive all the men in his family.

Pat was surprised at how quickly he recovered. In part, this was due to his presurgery exercise program. Prior to surgery, Pat generally worked out four to six days a week either officiating at women's basketball games or on his Nordic track. Pat knew that conquering his weight would make him a better referee.

Within a few days of his discharge Pat was back to work. He attended a basketball tournament from July 27 to July 30, officiating up to a few games a day. While he did feel quite weak at this first tournament, at that point, only three weeks out from his procedure, he had already lost 30 pounds. Within two months he lost 60 pounds. Things slowed down a bit after the first 60 pounds, but at the six-month point he had dropped a total of 90 pounds. Now almost two years after his gastric bypass, Pat has lost over 100 pounds.

Does he have any regrets? Not really. He does admit that he is not as strong as he was before the bypass. Before surgery, he could easily lift a 350-pound engine alone—now his maximum is about 200 pounds. This is a concession he is more than willing to make.

Pat is still trying to figure out all the things he can and cannot eat, and he still struggles with learning to eat more slowly and to take smaller bites. Fifty years of habits are hard to break.

Planning Checklist for Gastric Bypass Surgery

Please give me a checklist of things I need to think about and/or accomplish in order to be successful in losing weight using gastric bypass as a tool.

This is a very important request and can really serve as a summary of this entire book.

- Determine if you are a candidate for this procedure: Is your BMI in the right range? Are you mentally prepared for the emotional ups and downs that will occur following this surgery?

- Determine if you are ready to make the necessary changes in diet and exercise required for a successful outcome.

- Locate a bariatric surgeon in your area.

- Discuss the procedure with your primary care doctor and if necessary ask for a referral to a bariatric surgeon. Ask your primary care physician and possibly other physicians for a letter of support.

- Obtain insurance coverage.

- Attend an informational meeting at your chosen center.

- Complete your center's presurgery program. Such a program should include a thorough medical history and physical, a nutritional consultation, a psychological evaluation, and a number of preoperative blood tests, and possibly other studies such as a sleep study, stress test, and gallbladder evaluation. (There may be a weight loss requirement prior to surgery.)

- Prepare yourself emotionally and physically for surgery. Make sure you have support at home when you return from your hospital stay.

- It is also crucial to have close contact with your bariatric center after surgery. You will follow up initially with your surgeon and nutritionist and later with a general internist who is also typically part of the team. Your center is also likely to have a support group that meets once a month. Attending this can keep you motivated and in contact with other people who will be experiencing the same things you are experiencing.

- Finally, stay focused on your goal to become a healthier, leaner person. Be faithful to your new diet and exercise plan. Progress in your diet only as directed by the nutritionist at your bariatric center.

I hope that you now have the information that you need about the medical and psychological aspects of gastric bypass surgery. If you decide gastric bypass surgery is right for you, I wish you every success.

Sample Letter from Your Primary Care Doctor or Surgeon

To Whom It May Concern:
Re: Donna Smith (DOB 11/30/69)

I am writing to request coverage for gastric bypass surgery for my patient Ms. Donna Smith. Ms. Smith is a thirty-three-year-old woman who is 5'3" tall and weighs 295 pounds, giving her a BMI of 52. She already suffers from many obesity-related disorders including diabetes, hypertension, hyperlipidemia, and sleep apnea. She has also been diagnosed with polycystic ovary syndrome and has been unable to become pregnant. I believe all her obesity-related conditions will be markedly improved with gastric bypass surgery.

I have been following Ms. Smith since she was eighteen years old. In that time she has been on multiple diets. She was on the Weight Watchers program for a period of one year. During that time she lost 60 pounds but quickly regained it. She has tried the Jenny Craig program without success and was followed by our hospital dietitian for over twelve months with little improvement.

Ms. Smith has been a diabetic for the last eight years. She is currently treated with Glucophage (metformin), Actos, and a nighttime dose of insulin. Despite this triple drug regimen, her blood sugar remains relatively poorly controlled. Her most recent fasting blood sugar was 170 mg/dL and her HA1C was 8.0. I believe gastric bypass surgery would allow discontinuation of most if not all of her diabetes medications and allow full normalization of her blood sugar and HA1C.

Ms. Smith developed hypertension four years ago and is currently on a beta-blocker with relatively good control of her blood pressure.

As is frequently seen in diabetics, Ms. Smith has had difficult-to-control hyperlipidemia. Prior to beginning both Lipitor and Tricor Ms. Smith had the following lipid profile:

Total cholesterol: 290 mg/dL

Triglycerides: 590 mg/dL

HDL-C: 30 mg/dL

Direct LDL: 155 mg/dL

The combination of diabetes, hypertension, and hyperlipidemia puts Ms. Smith at very high risk for the development of premenopausal heart disease.

Following polysomnography one year ago, Ms. Smith was diagnosed with sleep apnea. Since her diagnosis she has been treated with C-PAP (continuous positive airway pressure). Ms. Smith has had a great deal of difficulty tolerating C-PAP, but has been reluctant to undergo uvulopalatopharyngoplasty (a surgical procedure designed to increase the pharyngeal lumen by resecting redundant soft tissue). Gastric bypass with resultant weight loss is likely to dramatically improve Ms. Smith's sleep apnea and would likely make surgery for sleep apnea unnecessary.

Finally, although Ms. Smith and her husband would like to have a family, they have been unable to conceive. Her infertility is likely the result of polycystic ovary (PCO) syndrome, which was diagnosed seven years ago. Numerous studies have reported successful pregnancies in women diagnosed with PCO syndrome following gastric bypass surgery.

In summary, I believe that most, if not all of Ms. Smith's obesity-related disorders would be fully corrected by gastric bypass surgery. There is little doubt that surgery will dramatically reduce her reliance on medications, will very likely allow restoration of fertility, and will greatly reduce the risk of future cardiovascular disease.

Please feel free to contact me should you require additional information or documentation of her dietary efforts.

Sincerely Yours,
Mary P. McGowan, M.D.

Appeal Letter

To Whom It May Concern:

I am writing to appeal the denial (dated September 3, 20XX) I received regarding coverage for gastric bypass surgery. After reviewing my policy and the current National Institutes of Health guidelines for surgical eligibility,* I have determined that I am a surgical candidate and should be covered.

Although my policy specifically denies coverage for medications to treat obesity, it says nothing about surgical treatment for morbid obesity. Given the fact that I am 5'3" tall and weigh 295 pounds (giving me a BMI of 52) and I already suffer from many obesity-related disorders including diabetes, hypertension, high cholesterol, sleep apnea,

---

*National Institutes of Health Guidelines for Surgical Eligibility:
1. A BMI of 40 or more, or in some cases a BMI over 35 in association with one or more major obesity-related medical or physical problems.
2. Failed all previous attempts at weight reduction by conventional means (diet, exercise, counseling, and weight loss medications).
3. No history of alcohol or substance abuse.
4. Realistic expectations of surgical outcome.

and polycystic ovary syndrome, I am clearly a candidate for surgery. There is little doubt that all of my obesity-related conditions will be markedly improved with gastric bypass surgery.

I have been obese since childhood and have been on multiple diets. I was on the Weight Watchers program for a period of one year. During that time I lost 60 pounds but quickly regained it. I have also tried the Jenny Craig program without success and was followed by a local dietitian for over twelve months with little improvement. During this time I was followed by Dr. Mary P. McGowan. I enclose copies of my weight loss and weight gain as documented by Dr. McGowan in my medical record. As can be seen, although I am able to lose weight with standard dietary interventions, I have been unable to maintain my weight loss.

I have been a diabetic for the last eight years. I am currently treated with Glucophage (metformin), Actos, and a nighttime dose of insulin. Despite this triple drug regimen, my blood sugar remains relatively poorly controlled. My most recent fasting blood sugar was 170 mg/dL and my HA1C was 8.0. Based on data reported by the American Society for Bariatric Surgery, it is likely that gastric bypass surgery would allow discontinuation of most if not all of my diabetes medications and allow full normalization of both my blood sugar and HA1C.

I developed high blood pressure four years ago and currently require metoprolol.

I also have a history of very high cholesterol and triglycerides. Prior to beginning both Lipitor and Tricor I had the following lipid profile:

Total cholesterol: 290 mg/dL

Triglycerides: 590 mg/dL

HDL-C: 30 mg/dL

Direct LDL: 155 mg/dL

Dr. McGowan has explained that the combination of diabetes, high blood pressure, and high cholesterol puts me at very high risk for the development of premenopausal heart disease. One year ago I began to experience sleepiness during the day. Dr. McGowan asked me to have a sleep study called a polysomnograph. The sleep study confirmed the diagnosis of sleep apnea. Since my diagnosis I have been treated with C-PAP (continuous positive airway pressure). I find C-PAP difficult to tolerate, but I am reluctant to undergo uvulopalatopharyngoplasty (a surgical procedure designed to increase the pharyngeal lumen by resecting redundant soft tissue) because I have been told by my pulmonologist (Dr. William Messanote) that gastric bypass with its attendant weight loss would likely make this procedure unnecessary. I enclose a letter (Exhibit A) from Dr. Messanote suggesting I consider gastric bypass as an alternative to uvulopalatopharyngoplasty.

Finally, although my husband and I would like to have a family, we have been unable to conceive. There is little doubt that my infertility is the direct result of polycystic ovary (PCO) syndrome, which was diagnosed seven years ago. My infertility specialist Dr. Shirley Galucki has informed me that there are numerous studies that have reported successful pregnancies in women diagnosed with PCO syndrome following gastric bypass surgery. I enclose a letter from Dr. Galucki (Exhibit B) indicating her belief that gastric bypass surgery would likely dramatically improve my chances of a successful pregnancy.

In summary, I believe that most, if not all of my obesity-related disorders would be fully corrected by gastric bypass surgery. There is little doubt that surgery will dramatically reduce my reliance on medications, will very likely allow restoration of fertility, and will greatly reduce the risk of future cardiovascular disease.

In light of this additional information, I hope you will reconsider my case and provide coverage for gastric bypass surgery.

Sincerely Yours,
Donna Smith

Useful Websites and Sources of More Information

General Information

American Society for Bariatric Surgery
7328 West University Avenue, Suite F
Gainesville, FL 32607
Phone: (352) 331-4900
Fax: (352) 331-4975
asbs.org

American Obesity Organization
obesity.org

Finding a Surgeon in Your Area

American Society of Bariatric Physicians
Phone: (303) 770-2526
asbp.org

Support Groups Online

obesityuncensored.com

Glossary

ACE inhibitors Angiotensin-converting enzyme inhibitors, a class of blood pressure lowering medications. These agents are especially useful for people with heart disease, diabetes, or kidney disease. Examples include: benazepril (Lotensin), captopril (Capoten), enalapril (Vasotec), fosinopril (Monopril), lisinopril (Prinivil, Zestril), moexipril (Univasc), quinapril (Accupril), ramipril (Altace), and trandolapril (Mavik).

Adrenaline A hormone produced by the adrenal gland. This hormone is also known as epinephrine and is produced at times of fright, excitement, or anger.

Aerobic exercise Exercise in which the muscles utilize oxygen (aerobic means "with oxygen") to burn both sugar and body fat. Examples include walking, running, swimming, skiing, and cycling.

Anaerobic exercise Exercise that is performed in short, intense bursts and does not utilize oxygen. Examples include weight lifting and sprinting.

Androgen A male hormone.

Anemia A condition in which the blood count is reduced. Symptoms may include shortness of breath and fatigue.

Angina pectoris Chest pain or pressure resulting from insufficient blood flow (and oxygen delivery) to the heart muscle—typically, the result of blockages within the coronary arteries. In some people angina is felt as arm, jaw, or neck pain.

Angioplasty *See* coronary artery balloon angioplasty.

Anorexia nervosa A condition seen most commonly in young women characterized by extreme fear of becoming obese. Persons with this disorder have an aversion to food and lose significant amounts of weight. This condition can be life threatening.

Anti-anginal A drug that relieves symptoms of angina (chest pressure, back pain, jaw pain, shortness of breath).

Antihypertensive A medication that lowers blood pressure.

Aorta The most important artery in the body. This blood vessel carries blood away from the left side of the heart. Many blood vessels including the coronary arteries spring from the aorta.

Arrhythmia An electrical disturbance in the heart rhythm that is often the result of underlying coronary artery disease.

Arteries Blood vessels that carry oxygenated blood away from the heart to the rest of the body. The only exception is the pulmonary artery, which carries oxygen-poor blood to the lungs from the right side of the heart.

Arthritis A disorder characterized by inflammation of a joint or joints.

Atherosclerosis A disease process that begins in childhood, characterized by the gradual buildup of plaque within the artery wall. Hypertension is a major risk factor for the development of atherosclerosis. Other risk factors include elevated cholesterol, cigarette smoking, diabetes, obesity, and sedentary lifestyle. Cholesterol is the major constituent of the plaque. When a plaque becomes unstable, it can rupture and lead to angina or a heart attack.

Atropine A medication used to increase the heart rate.

Bariatric surgery One of several surgical procedures designed to promote weight loss. All weight loss surgeries restrict the size of the stomach (restrictive procedures). In addition some weight loss surgeries also prevent the absorption of calories and nutrients by bypassing a portion of the small intestine. Examples include the Roux-en-Y procedure, vertical-banded gastroplasty, biliopancreatic diversion with duodenal switch, and gastric banding.

Beta-blocker A medication used to treat high blood pressure. Beta-blockers are also used in the treatment of angina and reduce the risk of heart attack.

Biliopancreatic diversion with duodenal switch This weight loss surgery is the classic malabsorptive procedure. This surgery does not dramatically reduce the size of the stomach, yet weight loss can be very significant. In fact, this procedure is used most commonly with people who need the most dramatic weight loss. Since the stomach is not dramatically reduced in size, people can eat more following this type of surgery than following restrictive surgery. In this procedure food bypasses contact with most of the duodenum and all of the jejunum. Instead, the very beginning of the duodenum (or first part of the small intestine) is connected directly to the ileum (last part of the small intestine), bypassing most of the duodenum and the entire jejunum. The pancreas and gallbladder have ducts that carry digestive juices and enzymes to the duodenum. These enzymes and digestive juices allow for the breakdown of the food we eat. Once food is broken down it can be absorbed in the duodenum and jejunum. Since this procedure prevents the digestive juices and enzymes in the duodenum and jejunum from making contact with food until almost the end of the ileum, food is simply not absorbed effectively. This allows dramatic weight loss to occur, but it also results in a number of complications.

Binge eating disorder (BED) Episodes of binge eating that occur at least two days a week for a period of about six months. In addition to consuming large amounts of food over a period of about two hours, binge eaters describe a sense of loss of control. Most binge eaters describe eating very quickly and feeling very full. Binge eaters usually eat alone and are very distressed by their own behavior. People with BED do not vomit and do not fast or exercise to excess to make up for the bingeing.

Body mass index (BMI) A measure of obesity calculated by dividing a person's weight in kilograms by his or her height in meters squared.

Bulimia Self-induced vomiting, typically following binge eating.

Bupropion (Wellbutrin, Zyban) An antidepressant medication that is also used in smoking cessation and may promote weight loss.

Bypass *See* coronary artery bypass grafting.

C-PAP machine (continuous positive airway pressure machine) A machine used to deliver oxygen to a sleeping person who suffers from sleep apnea.

Calcium channel blocker A type of medication used to treat high blood pressure. Calcium channel blockers are also used to treat angina and may reduce the risk of heart attack.

Cardiac Pertaining to the heart.

Cardiac catheterization *See* coronary angiography.

Cardiac rehabilitation program A thrice weekly, medically supervised exercise program attended by people with cardiac disease. Such programs also generally include advice on diet, smoking cessation, and stress reduction.

Cardiac risk factors Aspects of one's life that predispose to the development of cardiac disease. These include high blood pressure, elevated cholesterol, smoking, diabetes, family history of heart disease, obesity, a sedentary lifestyle, stress, elevated blood homocysteine, elevated lipoprotein (a), elevated C-reactive protein, being a male over the age of forty-five, or being a postmenopausal female.

Cardiac stress test *See* electrocardiogram.

Carotid arteries Arteries in the neck that arise from the aorta and carry blood to the brain.

Carotid endarterectomy A surgical procedure performed when the carotid arteries are occluded with cholesterol plaque.

Cataract A condition characterized by clouding of the lens of the eye. Most people with cataracts experience blurred vision.

Catheterization *See* coronary angiography.

Cerebrovascular Pertaining to the blood vessels serving the brain.

Cerebrovascular disease Blockages in the blood vessels serving the brain that can result in stroke.

Cholesterol A white waxy substance found only in products of animal origin, including egg yolks, meat, cheese, milk, and ice cream. Cholesterol is also produced by all the cells of the body, especially by the liver cells. Small amounts are necessary to make cell walls and hormones.

Claudication Pain in the lower extremities resulting from inadequate circulation.

Coronary angiography A procedure in which dye is injected into the coronary arteries via a flexible catheter (a thin, hollow plastic tube) to determine if these arteries have significant blockages.

Coronary artery An artery that supplies blood and oxygen to the heart muscle. Coronary arteries arise from the aorta. The major arteries include the right coronary artery and the left main artery, which quickly divides into the circumflex and left anterior descending arteries.

Coronary artery balloon angioplasty A procedure in which a thin catheter containing an inflatable balloon is used to open a blocked artery. A metal stent is often placed in the artery at the site of the blockage to prevent the artery from closing following an angioplasty.

Coronary artery bypass grafting Open-heart surgery in which a leg vein (saphenous vein) or breast artery (mammary artery) is used to connect the aorta with a coronary artery just beyond a blockage.

Coronary artery disease (CAD) A progressive disorder caused by blockages within the coronary arteries. Aftereffects of this disease include angina pectoris, heart attack, or sudden cardiac death. Individuals with CAD require lifestyle changes, risk factor reduction, and may require coronary artery bypass grafting or angioplasty.

Dexfenfluramine (Redux) A weight loss medication that was taken off the market in the late 1990s due to valvular heart disease and the potential deadly side effect of primary pulmonary hypertension (a restrictive lung disease).

Diabetes Repeated fasting blood sugar levels above 126 mg/dL.

Dialysis A procedure used in kidney failure to maintain electrolyte balance and to remove wastes and toxins from the blood. Hemodialysis is performed in a specialized center three times a week. Continuous ambulatory peritoneal dialysis (CAPD) is an alternative to hemodialysis performed by the person with kidney failure. CAPD involves instilling fluid into the abdominal cavity for several hours; the fluid is then drained, taking with it waste fluids and toxins.

Diastolic blood pressure The pressure in the body's arteries between heartbeats (as the heart is filling with oxygen-rich blood returning from the lungs).

Dobutamine A medication that makes the heart beat faster and stronger.

Dumping syndrome A syndrome caused by food passing quickly from the small stomach pouch into the jejunum. Symptoms include nausea, bloating, stomach cramps, and diarrhea. The dumping syndrome generally occurs after a person eats sweets. It is believed that part of the success of the Roux-en-Y procedure is due to the fact that when people find that eating sweets causes this problem they stop eating them.

Duodenum The first portion of the small intestine. Vitamin D, calcium, and nutrients are absorbed in this portion of the small intestine.

Echocardiogram A painless procedure that uses sound waves to assess heart muscle and valve function.

Edema Swelling of body tissue due to the buildup of salt and water. In most cases it is the ankles and lower legs that swell.

Electrocardiogram Often referred to as an EKG or ECG, an electrocardiogram is a painless procedure in which electrodes are placed on the chest wall, arms, and legs and used to monitor electrical impulses as they pass through the heart muscle, controlling its activity. In some situations an EKG is combined with exercise (a stress test). This is done to detect electrical disturbances that might not be evident at rest.

Endothelium The inner lining of an artery.

Esophagus The "food tube" connecting the mouth with the stomach.

Fat-soluble vitamins Include vitamins A, D, E, and K. Deficiency in these vitamins can result after some weight loss surgeries.

Fatty liver A condition in which the liver tissue becomes overloaded with fat cells; seen commonly in people who are obese and have diabetes or hypertriglyceridemia. Fatty liver often resolves with weight loss.

F.I.T. (frequency/intensity/time) principle The three things that must be kept in mind as a person develops an exercise program.

Gallstones Found in the gallbladder or bile duct and composed of cholesterol, calcium bilirubinate, and calcium carbonate.

Gastric banding Weight loss procedure that uses an inflatable silicone band to divide the stomach and create a very small stomach pouch. While the diameter of the band is generally about two inches (five centimeters), this can be adjusted by pumping saline into the band from a reservoir implanted under the skin. Blockage of the band can be problematic, and unfortunately the reservoir implanted beneath the skin doesn't last forever. Consequently, weight regain with this method frequently occurs. This procedure can result in iron and vitamin B_{12} deficiency.

Gastric bypass surgery A procedure used to treat morbid obesity. A small pouch is constructed between the esophagus and the intestines. The stomach is bypassed and the pouch serves as a new and very small stomach.

Genetics The study of heredity.

Ghrelin A recently discovered hormone that is secreted by endocrine cells within the stomach. Blood ghrelin levels rise prior to meals and in the face of food restriction or starvation.

Gout A disorder characterized by an elevated blood uric acid level and severe, recurrent attacks of joint pain (generally in the great toe) caused by the deposition of uric acid crystals in the connective tissues of the joint.

Heart attack *See* myocardial infarction.

Heart failure Frequently called congestive heart failure, this is a condition that occurs when the heart muscle is unable to adequately pump blood from the heart to the rest of the body. People with heart failure will often experience fluid buildup in the ankles, feet, and lungs. Heart failure can occur following a heart attack, especially when a large amount of heart muscle has been damaged.

Hernia Protrusion of intestine through the abdominal wall (in the case of an abdominal or umbilical hernia) or through the inguinal canal (in the case of an inguinal hernia). Abdominal hernias often occur following surgery involving an abdominal incision. Consequently, these hernias are often called incisional hernias.

High blood pressure *See* hypertension.

High-density lipoprotein cholesterol (HDL-C) Often referred to as the good cholesterol, high levels of this lipoprotein protect against the development of cardiac disease through a process called reverse cholesterol transport.

HMG CoA reductase inhibitor A class of cholesterol-lowering drugs including atorvastatin (Lipitor), lovastatin (Mevacor), simvastatin (Zocor), pravastatin (Pravachol), and fluvastatin (Lescol).

Hypercholesterolemia An elevated blood cholesterol level.

Hypercortisolism (Cushing's syndrome) A disorder characterized by the overproduction of cortisol from the adrenal gland. One of the findings in this disorder is high blood pressure.

Hypertension A condition characterized by sustained high blood pressure and an increased risk of heart disease, stroke, and kidney failure. While lifestyle changes such as salt and alcohol restriction, exercise, weight loss, and smoking cessation may normalize blood pressure, there are cases when medications are necessary.

Hyperthyroidism A condition in which the thyroid gland is overactive. This condition can lead to high blood pressure. Therapy may involve either medications or surgery.

Hypoglycemia Low blood sugar.

Hypothalamus The portion of the brain responsible for water balance, sugar and fat metabolism, and regulation of body temperature.

Hypothyroidism A condition in which the thyroid gland is underactive. This condition can lead to high blood pressure. Therapy involves daily thyroid replacement in the form of a pill.

Ileum The third and final portion of the small intestine.

Infertility Inability or reduced ability to become pregnant and deliver a live infant.

Insulin A hormone produced by the pancreas. This hormone promotes the entry of sugar into the cells.

Insulin resistance A disorder characterized by decreased responsiveness to the hormone insulin. As compared to people without insulin resistance, persons with this disorder must produce significantly larger amounts of insulin to maintain the same blood sugar level.

Ischemia An imbalance between the oxygen demand of a portion of the heart muscle and the oxygen supply delivered to that portion of the heart muscle. Ischemia is the result of a blockage within one or more of the coronary arteries.

Jejunum The second portion of the small intestine. This portion of the small intestine is responsible for calcium, vitamin D, and nutrient absorption.

Laparoscope A surgical instrument with a small light on the end. Weight loss surgery is frequently performed with the aid of a laparoscope.

Lipid A blood fat. Examples include LDL-cholesterol, HDL-cholesterol, and triglycerides.

Low-density lipoprotein cholesterol (LDL-C) Often referred to as the bad cholesterol, elevated levels of this blood fat increase the risk of developing heart disease.

Malabsorptive surgery A weight loss surgery in which a large portion of the small intestine is bypassed resulting in the inability to absorb calories. Most weight loss procdures have both restrictive and malabsorptive components.

Menopause The time in a woman's life when the ovaries cease to produce the female hormones estrogen and progesterone. In the United States the average woman enters menopause at about age fifty-one. Smokers tend to enter menopause at an earlier age.

Monounsaturated fat The type of fat found in canola oil, olive oil, and peanut oil. This type of fat is also present in avocados and peanuts. When this type of fat is substituted for saturated fat, total cholesterol level will fall and the HDL-cholesterol level may rise.

Myocardial infarction A heart attack. This condition develops when an area of heart muscle is deprived of oxygen. The result is cellular death and eventual scar formation.

National Institutes of Health (NIH) A large governmental organization that performs independent research, conducts national health surveys, produces consensus documents regarding disease states, and provides worthy scientists throughout the United States with research grants.

Normotensive Having normal blood pressure.

Obesity Having a body mass index (BMI) over 30. Class I obesity is defined as a BMI between 30 and 34.9; Class II and III obesity are defined as a BMI between 35 and 39.9 and greater than or equal to 40 respectively.

Obesity-related illness A condition or disorder that develops as a result of obesity. These include elevated cholesterol and triglycerides, gallstones, pancreatitis, abdominal hernia, fatty liver, diabetes and prediabetes, polycystic ovary syndrome, high blood pressure, heart disease, pulmonary hypertension, stroke, blood clots in the legs and lungs, sleep apnea, arthritis, gout, lower back pain, infertility, urinary incontinence, and cataracts.

Obstructive sleep apnea A disorder caused by airway obstruction during sleep and characterized by snoring, gasping, and apnea (lack of breathing) during sleep. Sleep apnea is associated with daytime drowsiness and high blood pressure. Therapy typically involves weight loss and alcohol restriction. At times facial appliances are utilized to prevent airway obstruction during sleep. Occasionally surgery will be required.

Orlistat (Xenical) A weight loss medication that works by preventing fat absorption.

Pancreas An endocrine gland that makes insulin and digestive juices. Digestive juices made in the pancreas flow through the pancreatic duct into the duodenum (first part of the small intestine). The pancreatic juices aid in digestion.

Peripheral vascular disease A disorder characterized by atherosclerosis of the lower extremities. The most common symptom of PVD is claudication or leg pain that occurs with walking.

Persantine sestamibi stress test A test used to assess the health of a person's heart without requiring exercise. Persantine is injected into a person's vein and makes the heart beat faster and more forcefully (mimicking exercise). Sestamibi is a nuclear isotope that finds its way into healthy heart muscle cells. This study takes about three hours to complete and requires both radiographic pictures and electrocardiograms.

Phentermine (Ionamin) A weight loss medication that works by suppressing appetite.

Pituitary gland A small endocrine gland found at the base of the brain. The pituitary gland secretes various hormones that serve to regulate many bodily processes including growth and reproduction and multiple metabolic activities.

Placebo An inert medication or sugar pill often used in research trials.

Plaque A blockage within an artery composed of cholesterol, cellular debris, inflammatory cells, and fibrous material.

Platelet Blood-clotting cell.

Pneumonia Infection in the lungs. Pneumonia caused by a bacteria typically requires antibiotics.

Polycystic ovary syndrome (PCO syndrome) A disease in which women fail to ovulate regularly. Some women with PCO syndrome fail to ovulate at all. The ovaries of women with PCO syndrome have many cysts.

Polyunsaturated fat The type of fat found in corn, sunflower, and safflower oils. When this type of fat is substituted for saturated fat, both total and HDL-cholesterol levels may fall.

Primary aldosteronism A disorder caused by a tumor in one of the two adrenal glands or caused by diffuse enlargement of both adrenal glands. One of the major findings in primary aldosteronism is high blood pressure.

Pulse Beating of an artery that can be felt with the fingers and used to determine heart rate. While there are many locations on the body where a pulse can be felt, the most common are the carotid (in the neck) and the radial (in the wrist).

Restrictive procedure A type of weight loss procedure in which the size of the stomach is dramatically reduced. Weight loss occurs because of the inability to consume more than very small portions. Most weight loss surgeries include both a restrictive and a malabsorptive portion.

Roux-en-Y procedure This surgical weight loss procedure (named after Cesar Roux, a Swiss surgeon) creates a very small stomach pouch, which is stapled horizontally, separating it from the rest of the stomach. In some cases the small stomach pouch is physically separated from the rest of the stomach. Initially the stomach pouch can hold about one to two tablespoons of food. The small intestine is cut near the beginning of the jejunum (second part of the small intestine), and the long portion of the jejunum is attached to the newly created small stomach. Food travels from the small stomach directly into the jejunum. Digestive juices and bile still enter the duodenum, but these juices do not meet the food until farther downstream where the portion of the intestines containing the digestive juices is reunited with the portion containing food. Since food is in contact with the digestive juices for less than the normal period of time, some malabsorption occurs. The Roux-en-Y is generally accepted to be the best and safest bariatric procedure.

Saturated fat The type of fat found in butter, cheese, whole milk, ice cream, white marbling in meat, and palm and coconut oils. This type of fat is known to increase cholesterol levels dramatically.

Sibutramine (Meridia) A weight loss medication that works by suppressing appetite.

Sleep apnea A disorder that primarily affects overweight people. The definition of sleep apnea is the complete cessation of airflow at the nose and mouth multiple times during an hour of sleep. Sleep apnea may be treated with a C-PAP (continuous positive airway pressure) machine, which delivers oxygen to a sleeping person. Symptoms of sleep apnea may include daytime sleepiness and difficulty concentrating.

Small intestine The portion of the gastrointestinal tract between the stomach and large intestine. The small intestine is responsible for the absorption of vitamins, minerals, nutrients, and calories. The small intestine is divided into three parts: the duodenum, jejunum, and ileum.

Spleen An abdominal organ that aids in fighting infections. This organ can occasionally be injured during weight loss surgery.

Stress test *See* electrocardiogram.

Stroke Partial or total loss of function of a part of the body due to brain damage resulting from an interruption of blood flow to the brain.

Syndrome X A dysmetabolic disorder characterized by high blood pressure, insulin resistance (prediabetes), and high blood triglycerides and low HDL-cholesterol (the protective cholesterol). This syndrome dramatically increases the risk for premature heart disease and has both a genetic and environmental basis.

Target heart rate The goal heart rate during exercise. In general the target heart rate is between 50 and 85 percent of a person's maximum heart rate (an easy way to calculate the maximum heart rate is to subtract a person's age from 220).

Triglyceride One of the blood fats. Triglycerides may be made by the liver or ingested through the diet. An elevated triglyceride level appears to be a strong predictor of developing heart disease, high blood pressure, and diabetes.

Ultrasound An inaudible sound used to produce an image or photograph of an organ or tissue within the body.

Vertical-banded gastroplasty Vertical-banded gastroplasty is a purely restrictive weight loss procedure. In vertical-banded gastroplasty the stomach is stapled fairly close to where the esophagus meets the stomach. The staples are placed in a vertical fashion and a polypropylene (plastic) band is placed near the bottom of the staple line. The stapling results in a very small stomach, while the band restricts how quickly food can leave this reduced pouch.

Vitamin B_{12} A vitamin found in food and supplements. Vitamin B_{12} is absorbed in the stomach. Deficiency can result in a disorder called pernicious anemia.

Weight loss surgery *See* bariatric surgery.

Wellbutrin *See* bupropion.

Zyban *See* bupropion.

Bibliography

Allison, D. B., et al. "Annual Deaths Attributable to Obesity in the United States." *Journal of the American Medical Association* 282 (1999): 1530–38.

Balsiger, B. M., et al. "Prospective Evaluation of Roux-en-Y Gastric Bypass as Primary Operation for Medically Complicated Obesity." *Mayo Clinics Proceedings* 75 (2000): 673–80.

Blackburn, G. L. "Managing Obesity in America: An Overview." *Johns Hopkins University School of Medicine: Advanced Studies in Medicine* 2 (2002): 40–49.

Brolin, R. E. "Bariatric Surgery and Long-Term Control of Morbid Obesity." *Journal of the American Medical Association* 288 (2002): 2793–96.

Brolin, R. E. "Gastric Bypass." *Surgical Clinics of North America* 81 (2001): 1077–94.

Byrne, T. K. "Complications of Surgery for Obesity." *Surgical Clinics of North America* 81 (2001): 1181–93.

Cariani, S., et al. "Complications After Gastroplasty and Gastric Bypass as a Primary Operation and as a Reoperation." *Obesity Surgery* 11 (2001): 487–90.

Cheskin, L. J. "Effective Strategies for Treating Obesity." *Johns Hopkins University School of Medicine: Advanced Studies in Medicine* 2 (2002): 38–39.

Choban, P. S., et al. "Bariatric Surgery for Morbid Obesity: Why, Who, When, How, Where, and Then What?" *Cleveland Clinic Journal of Medicine* 69 (2002): 897–903.

Contreras, J., and D. Noonan. "The Diet of Last Resort." *Newsweek*, June 2002, 46–47.

Cummings, D. E., et al. "Plasma Ghrelin Levels After Diet-Induced Weight Loss or Gastric Bypass Surgery." *New England Journal of Medicine* 346 (2002): 1623–30.

Deitel, M., et al. "Gynecologic-Obstetric Changes After Loss of Massive Excess Weight Following Bariatric Surgery." *Journal of the American College of Nutrition* 7 (1988): 147–53.

Field, A. E., et al. "Impact of Overweight on the Risk of Developing Common Chronic Diseases During a 10-Year Period." *Archives of Internal Medicine* 161 (2001): 1581–86.

Flegal, K. M., et al. "Prevalence and Trends in Obesity Among U.S. Adults, 1999–2000." *Journal of the American Medical Association* 288 (2002): 1723–27.

Fontaine, K. R., et al. "Years of Life Lost Due to Obesity." *Journal of the American Medical Association* 289 (2003): 187–93.

Foreyt, J. P., and G. K. Goodrick. "Weight Management Without Dieting." *Nutrition Today*, March/April 1993, 4–9.

Galuska, D. A., et al. "Are Health Care Professionals Advising Obese Patients to Lose Weight?" *Journal of the American Medical Association* 282 (1999): 1576–78.

Glazer, G. "Long-Term Pharmacotherapy of Obesity 2000: A Review of Efficacy and Safety." *Archives of Internal Medicine* 161 (2001): 1814–24.

Heymsfield, S. B., et al. "Recombinant Leptin for Weight Loss in Obese and Lean Adults: A Randomized, Controlled, Dose-Escalation Trial." *Journal of the American Medical Association* 282 (1999): 1568–75.

Higa, K. D., et al. "Laparoscopic Roux-en-Y Gastric Bypass: Technique and 3-Year Follow-up." *Journal of Laparoendoscopic and Advanced Surgical Techniques* 11 (2001): 377–82.

Holzwarth, R., et al. "Outcome of Gastric Bypass Patients." *Obesity Surgery* 12 (2002): 261–64.

Jakicic, J. M., et al. "Effects of Intermittent Exercise and Use of Home Exercise Equipment on Adherence, Weight Loss, and Fitness in Overweight Women: A Randomized Trial." *Journal of the American Medical Association* 282 (1999): 1554–60.

Janssen, I., et al. "Body Mass Index, Waist Circumference, and Health Risk." *Archives of Internal Medicine* 162 (2002): 2074–79.

Klein, S. "Medical Management of Obesity." *Surgical Clinics of North America* 81 (2001): 1025–38.

Kral, J. G. "Morbidity of Severe Obesity." *Surgical Clinics of North America* 81 (2001): 1039–49.

Kushner, R. "The Treatment of Obesity: A Call for Prudence and Professionalism." *Archives of Internal Medicine* 157 (1997): 602–4.

Manson, J. E., and S. S. Bassuk. "Obesity in the United States: A Fresh Look at Its High Toll." *Journal of the American Medical Association* 289 (2003): 229–30.

Manson, J. E., et al. "Body Weight and Mortality Among Women." *New England Journal of Medicine* 333 (1995): 677–85.

Marceau, P., et al. "Malabsorptive Obesity Surgery." *Surgical Clinics of North America* 81 (2001): 1113–27.

Mokdad, A. H., et al. "Prevalence of Obesity, Diabetes, and Obesity-Related Health Risk Factors, 2001." *Journal of the American Medical Association* 289 (2003): 76–79.

Must, A., et al. "The Disease Burden Associated with Overweight and Obesity." *Journal of the American Medical Association* 282 (1999): 1523–29.

National Heart, Lung, and Blood Institute. "Clinical Guidelines on the Identification, Evaluation, and Treatment of Overweight and Obesity in Adults: The Evidence Report." *Obesity Research* 6, suppl. 2 (1998): 51S–210S.

National Task Force on the Prevention and Treatment of Obesity. "Overweight, Obesity, and Health Risk." *Archives of Internal Medicine* 160 (2000): 898–904.

Nguyen, N. T., et al. "Laparoscopic Versus Open Gastric Bypass: A Randomized Study of Outcomes, Quality of Life, and Costs." *Annals of Surgery* 234 (2001): 279–91.

Nielson, S. J., and B. M. Popkin. "Patterns and Trends in Food Portion Sizes, 1977–1998." *Journal of the American Medical Association* 289 (2003): 450–453.

Norman, R. J., and A. M. Clark. "Obesity and Reproductive Disorders: A Review." *Reproduction, Fertility and Development* 10 (1998): 55–63.

Pories, W. J., et al. "Who Would Have Thought It? An Operation Proves to Be the Most Effective Therapy for Adult-Onset Diabetes Mellitus." *Annals of Surgery* 222 (1995): 339–52.

Saunders, R. "Compulsive Eating and Gastric Bypass Surgery: What Does Hunger Have to Do with It?" *Obesity Surgery* 11 (2001): 757–61.

Serdula, M. K., et al. "Prevalence of Attempting Weight Loss and Strategies for Controlling Weight." *Journal of the American Medical Association* 282 (1999): 1353–58.

Silverstone, T. "Appetite Suppressants." *Drugs* 43 (1992): 820–36.

Sjostrom, C. D., et al. "Reduction in Incidence of Diabetes, Hypertension, and Lipid Disturbances After Intentional Weight Loss Induced by Bariatric Surgery: The SOS Intervention Study." *Obesity Research* 7 (1999): 477–84.

Sugerman, H. J. "Effects of Increased Intra-abdominal Pressure in Severe Obesity." *Surgical Clinics of North America* 81 (2001): 1063–75.

Sugerman, H. J., et al. "Prophylactic Ursodiol Acid
    Prevents Gallstone Formation Following Gastric
    Bypass Induced Rapid Weight Loss: A Multicenter,
    Placebo Controlled, Randomized, Double-Blind
    Prospective Trial." *American Journal of Surgery* 169
    (1994): 91–96.

Surgeon General's Call to Action to Prevent and Decrease Over-
    weight and Obesity. Rockville, MD: U.S. Department
    of Health and Human Services, 2001.

Task Force on the Prevention and Treatment of Obesity.
    "Overweight, Obesity, and Health Risk." *Archives of*
    Internal Medicine 160 (2000): 898–904.

Tauber, M., and M. Dagostino. "100 and Counting."
    People, November 2002, 104–10.

Wadden, T. A., et al. "Psychological Aspects of Obesity
    and Obesity Surgery." *Surgical Clinics of North America*
    81 (2001): 1001–21.

Wannamethee, S. G., et al. "Weight Change, Weight Fluc-
    tuation, and Mortality." *Archives of Internal Medicine*
    162 (2002): 2575–80.

Wee, C. C., et al. "Physician Counseling About Exercise."
    Journal of the American Medical Association 282 (1999):
    1583–88.

Wei, M., et al. "Relationship Between Low Cardiorespira-
    tory Fitness and Mortality in Normal-Weight, Over-
    weight, and Obese Men." *Journal of the American*
    Medical Association 282 (1999): 1547–53.

Wittgrove, A. C., et al. "Pregnancy Following Gastric
    Bypass for Morbid Obesity." *Obesity Surgery* 8
    (1998): 461–64.

Yanovski, S. Z. "Binge Eating Disorder: Current Knowledge and Future Directions." *Obesity Research* 1 (1993): 306–24.

Yanovski, S. Z., and J. A. Yanovski. "Obesity." *New England Journal of Medicine* 21 (2002): 591–602.

Index